P9-CAD-532

Walking
Wisdom

Walking Wisdom

THREE GENERATIONS,
TWO DOGS, *and the* SEARCH
for a HAPPY LIFE

GOTHAM CHOPRA

with DEEPAK CHOPRA

HYPERION

NEW YORK

Copyright © 2010 Gotham Chopra with Deepak Chopra

All rights reserved. No part of this book may be used or reproduced in any manner whatsoever without the written permission of the Publisher. Printed in the United States of America. For information address Hyperion, 114 Fifth Avenue, New York, New York, 10011.

Library of Congress Cataloging-in-Publication Data has been applied for

ISBN 978-1-4013-1034-9

Hyperion books are available for special promotions, premiums, or corporate training. For details contact the HarperCollins Special Markets Department in the New York office at 212-207-7528, fax 212-207-7222, or e-mail spsales@harpercollins.com.

Book design by Chris Welch

FIRST EDITION

10 9 8 7 6 5 4 3 2 1

THIS LABEL APPLIES TO TEXT STOCK

To:

Krishu, Leela, Tara, Kiran, Noah, Alex, Aanya, Mira, Dakshu, Sumair, Cleo, and Nicholas. You're all my babies.

Thank you for all the love and licks.

acknowledgments

Like every great experience, the one that was writing this book evolved through a confluence of relationships and events.

First came the backdrop of my amazing family: the ever-evolving relationship and friendship with my father; the nonstop love and commitment from my mother; the long-distance care and compassion from my in-laws; the wisdom of my grandparents; the liveliness and laughter from my amazing wife, Candice, son, Krishu, doggy, Cleo, and memory of Nicholas; and the nurturing mentorship from my "other household"—Mallika, Sumant, Tara, Leela, and puppy Yoda.

Next up: the great folks of Trident Media Group, notably Robert Gottlieb and Eileen Cope, both of whom not only give agents a great name—a monumental and unique achievement—but are friends first and masterful mentors.

Brenda Copeland at Hyperion: you took this crazy idea about my dad and dog and helped mold it into something very special for me that I am so excited and proud to share with my family and the world. I'm forever grateful. Beyond that, your creativity within chaos has also forced me to develop a skill set I happily ignored for several decades—being organized. I guess I should be grateful for that too.

Last but certainly not least, I'd like to acknowledge my late friend Michael Jackson. He passed while this book was coming together. We struggled with how much to really include his presence in the book, to honor but not exploit, to commemorate but not clutter. I hope we did you right. Thanks for being a great friend and a real star. Rest in peace, Applehead.

Gotham Chopra

Walking Wisdom

introduction

OBSESSED. THERE WAS NO BETTER WORD FOR IT. WE WERE obsessed. When I was seven and my sister, Mallika, was eleven, all we could talk about—all we could think about—was getting a dog. I appreciate that as obsessions go, this one was hardly unique, that most kids are fanatical about dogs and cats, most families suffer through the phase. But when you're seven and every waking moment is taken up with this need—this desperate, urgent desire—well, the idea of a universal experience doesn't seem to matter. This wasn't some rite of passage. It was life or death. And we behaved accordingly.

Mallika and I nagged our parents morning, noon, and night. We moped. We pleaded. We cajoled. We made promises we knew we'd never keep. I offered to forgo my allowance in exchange for a kibble for work program, while Mallika swore she'd bathe the dog every day. We'd take care of the mess. We'd take care of the walks. We'd take care of everything.

"We'll look after the dog, Mom. Honest we will." That was me.

"You won't need to do anything at all. You'll hardly notice the dog even exists." That was Mallika.

My mom, always open to negotiating, took advantage of the

situation by horse-trading tasks she'd been fighting hard over for some time. My father, on the other hand, was unmoved. A hard-working physician with multiple jobs, he had no interest in our adding another being to our household, especially a four-legged one. Never what you'd call a "dog person," Papa looked at our neighbor's St. Bernard—an oafish, uncoordinated, sloppy, and constantly drooling beast—with open disgust. Hence he pretty much regarded all dogs as oafish, uncoordinated, sloppy, constantly drooling . . . and unintelligent to boot.

It might have ended there, but as was always the case in our family, once my mother had green-lit the enterprise, my father's opinion didn't really matter.

Mallika and I celebrated the imminent addition to our family.

The Chopras were getting a dog.

NICHOLAS WAS A blaze of energy and anarchy, a little Samoyed pup that was nothing more than a fluffy white ball of fur. We could hardly tell which end was up. Nicholas was goofy and playful and eager to please, but like most puppies, he was ill equipped to do anything quite right. So what if he peed where he wasn't supposed to? So what if he chewed a table leg, broom handle, or couch pillow? These actions only served to make him that much more lovable. No matter what he did, no matter what high jinks he got up to, Mallika and I were happy. Ridiculously happy.

How could we not be?

Our dream had come true: We had a puppy dog.

Nicholas spent most of his time barreling around the house, wrestling plush toys and those little bones that we'd pick up daily from the local pet store. He'd tear from one side of the house to the other with speed and cunning. When we finally tracked him down, he'd be hard at work ripping apart a pillow or another piece of furniture. Shoes were another favorite, as were the stuffed animals that sat in our bedrooms.

Bath times, which were frequent at the beginning when we naively thought we could keep him clean, were a sudsy bonanza that often concluded with Nicholas escaping. We'd follow the slick, soapy trail throughout the house from the book-cluttered den through the art-laden living room and usually to one of our bedrooms, where we'd find our pup chewing up a pillow or tearing apart one of Mallika's many pairs of jelly shoes.

"Oh well." She shrugged, prying away the ragged remnants before pulling Nicholas in for a cuddle. "It's no big deal."

It was indeed a big deal, considering how much my preteen sister loved her shoes.

"Nicholas is our baby," she assured me. "Nothing will ever compare to him."

And that pretty much summed it up. For both of us.

My father, meanwhile, tried to lay down the law. He insisted we keep Nicholas in the basement of the house, where we set up an elaborate playpen-slash-doghouse with food and water, toys and blankets, and, now that we knew he enjoyed them so much, an old pair of shoes. But all through his very first night with us, Nicholas whined and cried. His whimpers echoed throughout the house. None of us slept a lick. That first night in the basement turned out to be his last.

Over the next few months, Nicholas rapidly grew from a small white fur ball to a sizable and beautiful canine. Still, despite some halfhearted attempts at training, he never quite lost his puppy-like attitude. Nicholas was an oafish, uncoordinated, sloppy, and constantly drooling blaze of energy. He was my father's worst fears come true. But for the rest of us, it was love.

Nicholas was becoming a part of the family. Our three cousins who lived just fifteen minutes from our house in suburban Boston—and whom we regarded more as siblings than the strange American term of "first cousins"—came over almost daily so we could all romp and play with Nicholas. More anarchy.

My father, however, held the line. Nicholas was kept in a separate room during mealtimes and, unless Papa wasn't looking (in which case, Mallika and I would slip our boy a people ration), he only got to eat dog food. And while Nicholas had succeeded in escaping the basement, which Mallika and I now regarded as little more than a dungeon, he was only allowed to snuggle up with a dirty piece of laundry at the foot of either my or my sister's bed. Doctor's orders.

Despite his protests and obvious disapproval, in Nicholas Papa soon found another appeal. Even at our tender ages, both Mallika and I had learned to resist our father's experiments. From as far back as I can recall, he would practice some routine or ritual he'd recently read about on us: from hypnosis, to diet, to observing silence for hours at a time (to enhance our creativity, he claimed), to "communicating with the universe" via a Ouija board in order to propel us to higher consciousness, whatever that meant. Mallika and I were used to being Papa's test subjects, and we reacted with a mixture of annoyance and entrepreneurship. Mallika, always the math whiz, devised a sliding scale that, depending on the intensity of the experiment, required Papa to up our weekly allowance. She was also nice enough to maintain my accounts and charge me interest for doing so, a relationship I found reasonable.

Nicholas, on the other hand, was always up for a new game, especially if there was a reward like a bone or a doggy treat at the end of it. He'd show remarkable aptitude for learning a routine—from staying still to retrieving a ball to other forms of advanced Deepak

Chopra trials—only to quickly abandon them once he had received his prize. This created great frustration for my father, an admirer of the scientist Rupert Sheldrake, who pioneered many progressive theories on consciousness largely based on his study of animal behavior. On the contrary, Nicholas's behavior challenged Sheldrake and Papa's joint hypothesis that the evolution of intelligence and consciousness should not be dependent on a bone or a doggy treat.

"Darwin presumably had better test animals to work with," Papa said, frustrated.

I had no idea what he was talking about, but Mallika was all over it. "We could get another dog," she offered. "A trained dog. You know . . . so you could establish a variable."

"No thanks," Papa replied. The mad scientist in him was determined. "I'll work with what I have."

One of my father's long-standing intentions with Nicholas was for us all to recognize and appreciate our instinctive trust in one another. The embodiment of this, Papa claimed, would be in letting Nicholas off his leash and trusting that he would stay by our side and not run off. Mallika and I knew that other dogs had managed such a feat, that millions of dogs before Nicholas had been trained to stay by their owners' sides without the benefit of a leash. No big deal. And yet we were nervous.

Papa wanted to establish the remarkable power of trust, to prove to us that simply by showing love and trust in Nicholas he would love and trust us in return. "Trust is the basis of any nurturing and evolutionary relationship," he proposed. "Only with that basic and strong foundation can we then move on to the bigger stuff like nonlocal communication."

It sounded fishy to us. But who were we to question a man so confident in his wisdom? Who were we to question Papa?

So one New England autumn afternoon, when the leaves had turned our street a magnificent blaze of fiery orange and deep yellow, it was showtime.

Papa began by speaking to Nicholas the way he would any other member of our family. "In a few moments, I'm going to unhook the leash from your collar, okay?"

Nicholas stared at him with a blank expression. His chest heaved. His heart pounded. "We trust and love you and never want you to feel restricted," Papa continued. "And we know that you'll return that love and trust by staying close to us."

Nicholas played along skillfully as a gentle papa slowly unfastened the leash. "We trust you," he repeated. "We all trust you."

Nicholas stood for a beat, smiling ear to ear, a string of drool dripping from his mouth. To my father, Nicholas appeared a divine, if somewhat oafish, picture of innocence and obedience. Mallika and I knew better. Faster than you could say "limbic resonance," he took off out of sight.

I cried.

Mallika grew angry.

Papa appeared totally confused.

I remember it distinctly as the first time I had ever heard the word *reckless*, something Mallika had just learned in her first few days of junior high and now unleashed on Papa. He too was distraught, more so with the realization that his latest theory had gone so catastrophically off track than with any regard for the dog. We spent the next two hours traipsing through the woods, searching neighbors' yards and a nearby park, but there was no sign of Nicholas. We were devastated—as much for the loss of our beloved pet as for the growing recognition that we were going to have to break the news to our mother.

There is only one thing in life, I would learn years later, that rivals the instinct to protect your child from any sort of pain, and that is protecting your mother. The clock was ticking toward that end.

As we made our way home, Mallika and I stewed in our silence. We were convinced Nicholas was lost forever and we fully intended on staying angry with our father for just as long. But then, as we climbed the driveway that led to our house—and we did this slowly, so that Papa would understand with each heavy step the measure of our sadness—we saw my mother, and beside her, Nicholas. She smiled. We smiled. Relief washed over us.

"Mr. Casparian saw Nicholas swimming in the reservoir. Luckily he recognized him," Mom informed us as Papa grimaced. "Thank heavens for good neighbors."

She stroked Nicholas affectionately. His white coat showed evidence of dried blood, marks of a playful scrape with another dog. Mallika and I rushed to Nicholas's side and engulfed him with a barrage of affection.

"Don't you ever do that again!" I chastised Nicholas, digging my hands deep into his fur and going nose to wet nose with him so he knew I meant business.

"It's not his fault," Mallika reminded me, throwing an angry glance Papa's way. She buried kisses onto the top of Nicholas's head and rubbed his tummy.

"Did Mr. Casparian bring him home?" Papa inquired.

Mom shook her head. "He tried to but couldn't. Nicholas came home by himself."

Papa couldn't help but smile triumphantly. Years later when reminiscing about the incident, my father told us that Nicholas proved us all right that day—he was defiant and obedient at the same time. He demanded freedom, but he knew we were his family and purposefully and loyally returned home to us. More importantly, he had given us a tremendous gift: By putting the family through such worry, he ultimately brought us closer than we were before. Nicholas had taught us a great deal, Papa said. Not only about himself and his pure innocence of just *being*, but also about one another and ourselves.

"You know," Papa affirmed at dinner a few days after the frost between us had started to thaw, "maybe this dog has a lot more to teach us than we have to teach him."

Nicholas stared up at Papa with a big, goofy grin. He had earned his way to the table side during dinnertime and Mallika and I were free to offer him full food rations without fear of reprimand from Papa. It was, after all, Papa who had discovered that Nicholas had a fondness for pork chops.

AS FAR BACK as I can remember, every single day of my life someone somewhere has asked me what it's been like to have Deepak Chopra as a father. They want to know if I am a master practitioner of *The Seven Spiritual Laws of Success*. Or whether I am of *Perfect Health*, meditate all day, communicate exclusively nonviolently, know my *dosha* quotient, or if I am a perfect yogi—in summary, if I live the perfect spiritual life.

The answer, of course, is: *almost.*

Actually, it's NO.

I like to think of myself as relatively normal, someone whose mood is too often dependent on the Red Sox box score from the prior night, who stresses out over the private school vs. public school debate for my kid, and who fantasizes about switching careers and becoming a Top Chef Master someday. Admittedly, though, it has been a pretty wild ride. From the Bible to the biology of the human soul, the *Bhagavad Gita* to *The Great Gatsby,* my father always believed in exposing my sister and me to the deepest reservoirs of knowledge he could find. To that extent, we also met a lot of interesting people along the way, including seers, psychotics, and many a celebrity who during or after their fifteen minutes of fame became spiritually obsessed with our father, Deepak Chopra. There were also a few prophets we encountered along the way, some for peace and others, well, for profit. Many of them had valuable lessons to share, some . . . not so much.

Still, recently when someone again asked me what it was like to grow up with Deepak as Dad, I found myself telling them the story about Nicholas and some of the lessons we all drew from him, including most notably my father. Even more recently, I, my father, and my two-year-old son, Krishu, went on a walk in the neighborhood in which I live with our current dog, Cleo, and I found myself thinking about those days with Nicholas once more. Along the walk, at some point Krishu saw something in the distance and pointed toward it. Instinctively, my father and I looked toward where Krishu was pointing, while Cleo stared at his little finger.

Noticing this, Papa laughed to himself.

I asked him what was so funny.

"It's an example of the difference between humans and dogs," he said. "Dogs are rooted in the present moment. They don't worry about tomorrow or wallow in yesterday. They have total present moment awareness and one-pointed attention."

Papa pointed ahead, mimicking Krishu. "Humans, on the other hand, are always looking for meaning and significance in things, longingly gazing toward the horizon for some deeper explanation to existence."

Papa reached down and petted Cleo's fluffy head. He turned to

Krishu. "As you become a big boy, we're all going to learn things from one another. Cleo too."

"Dada!" Krishu smiled, an affirmation of Papa's tenderness.

THESE DAYS, WHEN I THINK of the many influences in my life, the usual suspects rise to the top: teachers and mentors, friends, siblings, significant others, business partners, even adversaries and rivals who have managed to drop important lessons along the way. But amidst them all, three beings crystallize. One, predictably, is my dad. The others, not so predictably, are my dogs.

My dad has taught me about wisdom, curiosity, open-mindedness, and the richness of having a relentless passion for knowledge. My dogs, Nicholas and Cleo, have taught me about simplicity, innocence, devotion, and true spiritual freedom. And there are more qualities that I've learned from them: loyalty, trust, forgiveness, and the desire to play. The more I asked around of others, the more I learned that they too had learned great (dare I say *spiritual*) lessons from their canine companions.

Most recently, like countless before me, I have embarked on a new and critical path in life: parenting. I'll forgo all of the usual clichés about how my life changed the day I saw my son born. Seeing my child actually emerge from the womb was not high on my priority list. I was perfectly happy to wait outside the delivery room and receive the joyous news with a pat on the back and a cigar. But I did the right thing. I stayed beside my wife, Candice, holding her hand and saying what I hoped were comforting and encouraging words. Still, this so-called miraculous event didn't affect me the way I thought it should. (Watching the 2004 Red Sox beat the Yankees in Game 7 after being down three games to none, or seeing the New England Patriots win the Super Bowl against the St. Louis Rams in Super Bowl XXXVI—now those were miracles.)

Maybe I'm a slow learner, but it wasn't until a few months in, as I watched my son slowly transform from that gooey alien life into an infant driven by survival instincts into a real human being flooded with consciousness, that it hit me: I'm going to have to think about the values that I'm going to impart to my child.

For me, it was literally an awakening, a flicker in my own consciousness. There I was, having been exposed to so much my whole life, having access to my father—surely I needed to tap that well. Meanwhile, I also reflected more on all of my dealings with Cleo. From the time Candice and I first got her—a lonely rescue mutt with "food issues"—Cleo has been a wellspring of life lessons, delivered in a way that only her family could ever decipher or appreciate. At least, that's what we told ourselves.

With all that in mind, I decided a meeting of the minds was in order. One Sunday I brought my dad and my dog together, brewed some coffee, and cracked open a bag full of treats (Greenies for Cleo and brownies for Papa and me). My goal: to see if my dad's and my dog's philosophies on life aligned. We talked about Nicholas and Cleo, some of the more memorable events from their lives and the qualities we observed and admired most in them. The result is this book.

As we laughed at our memories, my father reminded me that many of the qualities we were enumerating were not only largely instinctive to dogs, but also generally present in humans.

"If anything," my father told me as we started to dig deeper into the idea, "we often create barriers that neutralize these instincts. To identify and nurture these qualities in our dogs is to cultivate them in our own lives, which ultimately helps us feel more fulfilled every day we exist.

"There is a genealogy to all of this," my dad continued, unable to resist the temptation to veer into his favorite arena of science and evolution. "Google it," another of his favorite expressions these days. "Tens of thousands of years ago, wolves and humans competed for food. But over time, that relationship transformed. Former foes became friends as the two species recognized in each other kindred spirits. Wolves—the genetic predecessors to dogs—live in family units just like we do, with two parents and a small number of pups."

Turns out he's right. The journey toward dogs becoming our best friends all started roughly between 12,000 and 15,000 years ago. We're talking hunter-gatherer time here for both humans and wolves, well before human settlements began appearing and our early agricultural culture set in. As part of our "civilized process," humans began cooking meat over fire. The aromatic smell drew certain wolves toward these early settlements. When the human residents discovered that some of these wolves weren't so threatening and might in fact prove to be helpful in accomplishing certain tasks, they freely offered up some of the meat to keep the wolves happy. Over time, a true codependence evolved: Packs of wolves and groups of nomadic men went out hunting together. The trade-off: With their superior smell and speed, wolves proved to be tremendous assets in tracking potential kills. In exchange, back at camp, humans cooked the meat and fed the wolves. An added bonus: The wolves—knowing where their bread was buttered, or in this case, where their steak was grilled—proved to be great guards against whoever might jeopardize this convenient arrangement they'd formed with their benefactors.

In time, this marriage of convenience transformed as many do into a genuine "love marriage," as my grandparents call it. Between that ancient wolf and the dog sitting at your feet came the interim evolutions of defender, watchdog, and shepherd. In short—actually over several millennia, but who's counting—the loyal domesticated dog with whom we form our inseparable emotional bonds has maintained many of the qualities and instincts of that original wolf searching for cooked meat. Go ahead and test it with a medium-rare T-bone. You'll see what I mean.

Take it a step forward, or backward in this case, and you can identify the connections we have with our dogs. My father now recalled some of the many articles he read back when we first got Nicholas and he aspired to become an immediate dog expert. "Dogs can read us—our behavior—and figure out what we want. They can read human social cues. It's pretty remarkable considering that even the chimpanzee, our closest animal relative with whom we are genetically aligned to the tune of ninety-six percent, cannot understand some of our gestures the way a dog can."

Again the research and genesis of humans and dogs reinforces this. As humans and dogs evolved together over thousands of years, the ability to communicate with us became part of dog DNA.

"Quite simply," my father concluded, "dogs became our best friends not by some random accident, but because of a relationship that evolved over time. Physical needs, emotional needs, psychological needs—we filled them for dogs and they filled them for us." My father turned to me. "Sounds like a pretty healthy relationship to me."

Here's the simple stuff: Dogs make us physically healthier by making us exercise. They make us emotionally healthier by asking for caresses that soothe not just their bodies, but our souls as well. The mere act of petting a dog can lower blood pressure. Seriously— go conduct your own experiment. And for many people, taking their dog for a walk—if even on a city sidewalk—is as close to nature as they get.

Talk to the experts: While different breeds have been designed for different purposes—from retrievers designed to help fishermen retrieve their catch to herding dogs who work with livestock to toy poodles designed solely for their companionship and lap-friendly size—all dogs have the universal ability to communicate with humans.

But is it possible to take this relationship to the next level?

To make it spiritual?

THE GREATEST LESSON I've learned from my father over the years is "Never take yourself too seriously." Of course, in our culture, we have a tendency to do the exact opposite, to quickly and fanatically build ideas around people and expectations of them, and then be disappointed when they fail to meet them. Often, we then topple those same pedestals on top of which we just placed someone.

Living and working in Hollywood, where pretty young actresses looking for their big break are plentiful, the expression "Men are dogs" is all too accurate. As a happily married man and father, I like to think of myself separate from this lot, and yet I know I too am a dog underneath. Not simply because at times I seem to be hormonally driven, but because I am an instinctive animal capable of raw emotion and primal behavior, as well as love, loyalty, emotional intelligence, and deep introspection. I contemplate things— like how to live a better life, how to contribute meaningfully to society, how to raise my son and care for my parents—and I like to think I am always willing to listen to some valuable advice. I am not presumptuous to think I know it all, no matter who my father is, especially when he tells me that he's got a long way to go himself.

"I try not to live my life worrying about what others think. A core spiritual quality is nonjudgment, which is not just about not judging others, but also not living your life worried about others judging you."

I was reassured. We were on our second pot of coffee.

"One more thing," my father added. "Spirituality does not start and stop. It's a ubiquitous part of life, in every moment, every encounter and relationship. Every nook and cranny of our lives is filled with the unfolding experience of self."

He grabbed a treat and handed it to Krishu, who ordered Cleo to sit and then rewarded her with it. My father smiled. In his interactions with my son, I sometimes sense he is in fact doing it the way he would with me if he were doing it all over again.

"All of our interactions with each other should be filled with meaning and significance." He nodded. "What could be more spiritual than that?"

one

Are you a dog person, Papa?

I'm supposed to say yes, right?

Right.

Yes, I am. I was not a dog person until you guys showed up.

And?

And . . . the more I'm learning about animals in general, the more I'm understanding that most of them are emotional beings. They form social hierarchies. They build closely knit and nurturing bonds with their offspring. They sing and play. And some have a degree of awareness, almost to the point of self-awareness such that they have a sense of humor. Animals and humans also form special connections through limbic resonance, cementing their physiological and emotional well-being. Mammals have a limbic brain and develop emotional and spiritual relationships with us. I probably should spend more time with animals.

IN MY FAMILY, THE FAMILY IS THE THING. WE ARE PRO-foundly close. I live a block and a half from my sister. I take my son to her house for breakfast pretty much every morning. Our families have dinner together about three days a week, and at least once over the weekend. Our children refer to each other as siblings and not just to each other. "Cousins" is an awkward term to them because it implies an emotional distance beyond brother and sister, which is how they've felt about one another from the moment they entered the world.

Mallika and I grew up much the same way with our so-called cousins. Even though we are separated by continents, we still refer to one another as siblings. Growing up with so many "brothers" and "sisters" was a thrill. Entire generational factions formed amongst older siblings, younger ones, tomboyish ones, girly ones, sporty ones, geeky ones, and so on and so on. Splinter groups formed between baseball fans and cricket fans, football fans and *fútbol* fans—there was even the Barbie bloc, with Diwali Barbie facing off against Malibu Barbie.

These days, most of us have gone beyond those mere surface differences to once again count ourselves as siblings. And now our kids, who I suppose are technically "second cousins," refer to each other as siblings too.

When it comes to adults, the same familiarity applies. Mallika and I call my father's younger brother "Chota Papa," which in Hindi means "small papa." His children call my father "Bara Papa," or "big papa." All of this can cause considerable confusion around the dinner table. Tara—Mallika's older daughter, a little more than eight years old and one of the elders of this generation—recently fielded the question from one of her classmates: *Are Indians like Mormons?* The girl had heard Tara reference the exploits of her countless "brothers" and "sisters."

"You mean like on the HBO show?" Tara responded.

And about "big papa," in this case the guru otherwise known as Deepak Chopra. Mallika and I have always called him "Papa." We never really got into the whole "Dad" thing. These days both of us talk to Papa at least four to five times a day. We are the reason wireless carriers created family calling plans. You're welcome.

But there really is only one anchor in the family. Mom. We've often joked that while my father talks it, my mom walks it. He may be great at coming up with lessons and laws that solve everything from stress management to existential madness, but it's Mom's grace, compassion, selflessness, and softness that are a shining example to everyone she comes into contact with. I am clearly my father's child—a dreamer, a creator, a wanderer with hopeless impatience and driving ambition—but the reason I am the way I am goes far beyond genetics. The mere fact that I've made it this far, succeeded in finding an amazing woman to be my wife, and together with her started a family, is due to the emotional tapestry that my mother has woven. She's the one, not only in our immediate family, but also all throughout our extended family and our many siblings, who provides the emotional bedrock on top of which we all stand. When *the shit hits the fan*, no one calls Papa for advice. We call Mom.

So in May of 2009, when my mom got a call that her father had been admitted to the hospital, it took her just five minutes to contact the travel agent and book her flight to New Delhi.

Nana, as we called him, had been on his early morning walk when he collapsed.

New Delhi in May is feverishly hot—intolerably so—with temperatures in the triple digits at the crack of dawn. Despite this, both my nana and my grandmother, Nani, insist on going on their daily walks. Of course, considering that they are both almost ninety and still active, it's hard to argue that they should let up on their routine. (That routine, by the way, involves their going on separate walks at separate times so they can meet up with their respective cronies and gossip while they stroll leisurely around the circular park.) Nana, in particular, brings a dry realism to these walks, as he does to most everything else at this stage of his life. Often when we talk on the phone he will tell me about the latest member of the group who has failed to show up. No further explanation required.

Nana and the rest of his buddies accept each absence with a stark detachment that is both ironic and comical. They are resigned to their stage of life and watch and comment on the world with this in mind.

"I don't know why we even tolerate Pakistan," Nana had remarked to me on a recent trip to India. Politics—especially its role in the strained relationship between India and its neighbor—is a constant source of discussion and debate for Nana.

"Maybe because it is a nuclear power," I proposed. "And any act of aggression could quickly escalate to something far more dangerous."

Nana waved his hand dismissively. "That would take years to happen." Years, Nana had clearly calculated, in which he would likely leave us.

Nana has been preparing for his own demise for some time now, something not uncommon within his group of buddies. Nevertheless, because the walkers take the narrow path two at a time, their fleet requires recalibration when one of their crew fails to show.

"It's not easy," Nana once told me. "Who walks alongside whom depends on who is a talker and who is a listener. Take Ramesh," he said, referring to a friend he'd had for close to forty years. "He passed away two months ago. Well, Ramesh walked with Arun, and he's always rattling on about this, that, and the next thing. No one wants to walk with that fellow, so now I have to."

"Your grandfather says he likes to listen," Nani interrupted us. "But he's only doing it because he's losing his hearing."

Nana smiled and nodded. Indeed Nani knows all his tricks.

Because he walks every day, we like to take Nana a new pair of sneakers when we visit him in India. But since Nana has been convinced for roughly the last decade that he's going to die imminently, he now refuses to accept new sneakers, which, he believes, will be wasted on him. He's nothing if not frugal. Since I have the same shoe size as Nana, I will often wear a new pair of kicks for about a week . . . or until they are no longer *new*. I'd gotten used to skidding through dusty construction sites, moonwalking down grimy parts of Hollywood Boulevard, or doing my best Kobe Bryant imitation on the Venice Beach basketball courts before packing them into a box that doesn't match their brand. All this so that Nana can accept the shoes with minimal guilt.

But for this trip my mom didn't have the usual time to gather gifts and plan her trip. As she rushed to gather her things in San Diego, where my parents have a home, she called to say she would be leaving from LA the following morning.

"Gotham," she said, waiting a beat, "I may be gone for a while this time."

"Okay," I murmured back on the phone. "We'll be fine, I think."

"Yes, you'll be fine. Candice takes care of everything," she said warmly.

The moment lingered.

"It's your father I'm worried about."

. . .

AS FAR BACK as I can recall, my father has always worked, and worked hard. Chief of staff at a prestigious local hospital and an associate professor at an equally highbrow university in Massachusetts where we grew up, he focused on moving forward with a singular fixation on his own professional path. Somewhere along the line, this obsession took a more spiritual shape, and his life and ambition were transformed. No longer part of the traditional medical community, he pioneered a new one that bridged conventional treatment with the ancient healing wisdoms of the past. As he blazed a trail through that wilderness, at times called out by cynics, skeptics, traditionalists—and dare I say racists—he did it with a passion and zeal that may suggest he was impervious to their rants. But he wasn't. So even as Mallika and I struggled to maintain some level of normalcy to our lives in suburban Boston, where being the children of an Indian doctor was unique enough, let alone one who was gaining notoriety for talking about such quasi-fringe practices as yoga and meditation, it was my mom who stood loyally by my father's side.

It was the commitment she had signed on for when the two of them were married when he was twenty-four years old and she was twenty-two. It was the commitment she had determined to honor. Within months of their marriage in India, my parents took off to a new life in glamorous Plainfield, New Jersey. They built that life in earnest, my father working all day in the hospital and then moonlighting in the emergency room on the night shift. Within a month, they bought a color TV and a Volkswagen Beetle, and the rest was history. Sure, there were a few bumps along the road, but nothing too catastrophic. And here they were almost forty years later.

So as my father gained acceptance through many of those years for the work he was doing, traveling to every corner of the globe to speak and teach, it was Mom who reminded him where he had come from, and equally important, where he was to come back to.

Later that evening, my parents arrived in Los Angeles. We all got together at Mallika's house for dinner. The most recent word from India was that Nana had stabilized but was still unconscious in the hospital. His heart was weak and he might need bypass surgery. His age, however, made the decision less certain. My mother's older sister was hopeful my mom would be there soon to help—check that—to *make* the decision.

"Is Bara Nana [big nana] going to die?" Tara asked as we silently ate dinner that night. My mother looked at her with tears in her eyes.

"No, Bara Nana will be just fine," Papa said, holding his grandaughter's gaze.

"Can I have strawberry milk?" little Leela (Tara's younger sister) asked. Since birth, she's had a knack for timing and getting the things she wants, including knowing when the adults' defenses were down.

"Sure." My sister nodded and got up to retrieve the milk.

"I want strawberry milk," little Krishu piled on, always echoing his older sister, whom he worships.

Mallika glanced at Candice, who shrugged her approval.

"I can make more saag curry," my sister's husband kindly offered, noticing the somber tone around the table. He's the undisputed top chef in the family. Like in most Asian clans, good food is the way we navigate through life's ups and downs. But not tonight. Our appetites were clearly off.

"No thanks." My mom got up from the table. "I'm going to call India again and check in."

Later, after the kids had gone to sleep and my father drifted outside on a phone call, my mother drew Mallika and me together again. "Your father will be fine. He's used to being alone. But this time, just stay in touch."

Ironic really, considering that on a normal day we're in touch close to half a dozen times.

"You know what I mean," she said.

We did know what she meant. With my mom having to hustle into action and get onto a plane with no real preparation and no definite plan to be back anytime soon, the fact was that my father was going to have to recalibrate considerably. He's quite adept at fending for himself, considering the amount of time he travels, speaking, teaching, and promoting his books. Less his physical whereabouts and movements, it was more his emotional anchoring my mother had in mind.

"Don't worry about it, Mom," Mallika advised her. "Just go take care of Nana."

My mom's eyes welled up again with tears. She nodded and then reached into her bag and pulled out a shoe box with a Nike swoosh plastered across its top. She lifted the lid to reveal a shining new pair of K-Swiss sneakers in my size. She handed them over to me.

"Go run around in these."

two

Father or grandfather? Which is your favorite role?

I think my favorite role is grandfather. When I was a father, I was so busy and so unaware that your mom had to take care of everything. But now, even though she still takes care of everything, I have more time to play. Or I should say, more inclination to play.

Wait—you're still a father!

Yeah, but my playful role comes from being a grandfather.

SATURDAY AFTERNOON. CANDICE WAS PUTTING KRISHU down for a nap, a weekend ritual that usually culminated in their both taking an afternoon slumber, while Cleo and I kicked back on the couch to take in whatever game we could find on television. Today though, I felt an awkward pressure to socialize with my father.

"What are you doing?" I asked him.

"Wikipedia," he said as he hunched over his computer, not taking his eyes off the screen. My father loves Wikipedia and Google. I mean serious infatuation. Keep that in mind as you read his next best seller. A vast wellspring of wisdom and knowledge, he is profoundly influenced by the two broadest information sources online.

"What are you reading about?" I pressed on.

"Happiness," he answered, clearly not feeling the same obligation I did.

"What about it?" I egged him on.

"Like all emotions, happiness creates a biological response. It triggers the release of specific chemicals in the brain in the perfect dosage, better than any pharmacy ever could. Fascinating."

Not really, I thought.

He sensed my dissatisfaction. "All animals including us create our own biologies. We dictate the quality and longevity of the life we live. Whether you have high counts of serotonin, an antidepressant drug, or cortisone, an anti-inflammatory, coursing through your body determines everything—how you feel about yourself, your work, your relationships, your life. If you can self-regulate those chemicals in your body without the aid of any drugs, then you control fully the quality of your life."

"Interesting." I decided to be the aloof one this time.

Surveying the situation and sensing that this was where we were hanging for the next few hours, Cleo moved toward my father, slid beneath his feet, did a few circles, and set down into a comfortable heap. He eyed her suspiciously.

"Don't mind her," I said. "She just wants to hang out near you."

"Why?"

I shrugged. "Because that's what makes her happy, I guess." Take that, Wikipedia.

"How old is Krishu?" my father inquired, taking his eyes off Cleo.

This is a unique quality of my father's. He's taken the idea of *time just being a concept* to a whole new level. Recently someone asked him how old I was. He eyed me like a technician surveys a lab rat in a cage and answered confidently, "Twenty-five." Being that I am thirty-four and his son, I'm not quite sure how to rationalize that one, except that maybe shorting me by a decade or so somehow made him feel younger. With Krishu, there is not that much time to play with. He's been with us for just short of two years. Though he appears to have laid out a hefty down payment on his terrible twos, at that moment he was pushing just about twenty months.

"Almost two," I answered my father. "Why?"

"We still have time," he said, sounding more and more like a mad scientist. "By the age of two, most children's brains are almost fully formed. By the age of four, their responses to various stimulae are so rigid, they can't be changed. By the age of eight, their neural pathways are so defined, their behavior patterns so fixed, there's hardly any point anymore."

He looked up at me. "Did you know that most leaders in the world—almost all men, incidentally—have the psychology and biological responses of eight-year-old boys? Threaten them and they threaten you back louder. Hit them and they hit you back harder. In that way, they are no different than little boys or dogs."

I furrowed my brow at him. Likewise at the mention of the word *dog*, Cleo perked. Where was he taking this?

Don't get me wrong. Similar sentiments had been plaguing me in recent months as I had seen Krishu's transition from an infant who relied solely on his mother for survival to an actual human being whose mind was in constant and rapid expansion. For the first eighteen months of his life, I had concluded that I was of little more value than a utility player is on a championship baseball team: I got the occasional pat on the back for surprisingly adding value, but those same folks would hardly notice if I were replaced by another body. The true participants in Krishu's evolution had been a gaggle of women: Candice, her mom, my mom, various "lactation consultants," and other moms with shared experiences. Let's not forget the online mommy tutors.

But then, around the eighteen-month mark, all of a sudden that baby started to become a kid. I, for one, found it intimidating and was still feeling the burden of it as I sat there with my father, sensing that he was preparing to start his experiments on my progeny. Candice had spent her full nine months of incubation reading every child development book known to man, and then reread them all when Krishu arrived, seemingly turning herself into a Jedi master of motherhood. But I had faltered, relying on the notion that some primal paternal instinct would kick in and navigate me through the maze of parenthood.

Whoops.

Now I eyed my father the same way that he eyed Cleo. Could he really be relied upon to offer me the wisdom I craved? I turned out okay, I thought to myself. Didn't I?

At that moment, Candice and Krishu pushed through the door into the living room. Krishu had a huge smile on his face and his mama looked weary. "He's not going down for a nap today. Too much excitement with Dada here."

On cue, Krishu sprinted across the room toward my father. "Dada!" he sang, plunging into my father's legs just as Cleo narrowly avoided his uncoordinated rush.

I might still be feeling out this father thing; nevertheless, I had adapted to the husband thing fairly well over the last seven years. Looking at Candice and sensing her fatigue, I turned back to my father and Krishu and grabbed Cleo's leash from the wall. "Why don't we all go for a walk?"

Krishu had just discovered the functionality of his legs in the last few months and the glorious act of walking that goes with it. Just strolling around our suburban Californian block is a real adventure for him. What should take about five minutes often turns into a twenty-five-minute odyssey so that he can reposition the white rocks that groom a neighbor's garden, smell the lemons hanging off the branches in another yard, point out the colors of cars that line the streets, and the crowning moment of every stroll—play fetch with Riley, the golden retriever who sits devotedly in front of her house waiting for whoever may pass.

I am reminded on these daily walks that neither of the two dogs I've had in my life—Nicholas nor Cleo—has ever mastered the game of fetch. I'm not sure if that's more a reflection on them or on my family's inability to teach the most simple and common game between a dog and its owner. Riley, on the other hand, is an expert fetcher. A handful of bald tennis balls always surrounds her. Using her snout she'll push them beneath her white picket fence, hoping to prompt a game of fetch with anyone who happens to walk by. Krishu, of course, is always game.

When I brought this up with my father—our dogs' historic inability to play fetch—he frowned and replied: "Training any animal, be it a dog or a human, to react in a Pavlovian manner, to grunt, pant, or drool on demand, is no great achievement."

"It's kind of a nice tradition," I offered, recalling all of the beer commercials I'd seen in which men and their dogs joyfully played fetch. Admittedly, I struggled to see Papa cast in that role.

Papa countered: "In fact, one of the greatest attributes that dogs have is their ability to just *be* without worrying about repercussions. That's a quality that should be nurtured in them."

Leave it to Papa to be the contrarian. Without even trying, I had rubbed him the wrong way. He started up again as we rounded the corner and ambled toward Riley's house. Krishu ran up excitedly a few feet ahead, anticipating the game.

"It's one of the significant problems we have in our society. We demand conformity, that people react how we want them to, meet our rigid expectations of them. As a result, they do. The average human has ninety thousand thoughts every day. Do you know that the vast majority of them are the same thoughts they had the day before?"

In fact, I did know that. Not because I'm some sort of behavioral scientist, but because I've been around my father enough to know that he often relies on the same statistics and examples to emphasize his theories. Ironic really, considering the point he was trying to make. I chose not to highlight this back to him.

He continued: "How often do leaders around the world react with anything other than absolute predictability? Agitate them and they react with suspicion, defensiveness, and hostility. It's the history of the planet and leads to greater distrust, confrontation, and war. I'd say that many of the leaders you see around the world—from presidents to prime ministers, dictators and demigods—are not that much more sophisticated than a dog playing fetch. Throw the ball, and get the expected result. The only problem now is that along with these ancient habits, we have modern technologies."

He huffed and shook his head. For the last few years, contrary to his reputation as a New Age savant in pursuit of answers to only existential angst, my father's main focus has been on global issues of war, social injustice, and the decaying ecology. Truth be told, he spends more time these days contemplating conflict resolution than karma, terrorism than timelessness. As he's entered what he so ominously calls the "twilight of his life," he's become obsessed with fixing the planet's physiology and biology, rather than healing its soul. As there is a lot of work to be done in that regard, I often find him frustrated and even despondent over something he's seen in the news. His greatest disappointment is with the lack of leadership around the world. It's a recurring theme with him.

"Give the leader of a toppled state a little authority and what does he demand? More. Rebuild the military or economy of a budding nation and what do they want? To become a superpower."

Papa shook his head ruefully. "Most so-called leaders around the world are petty tyrants, operating from the consciousness of pre-adolescent boys, without the ability to think outside of their own limited instinctive rigid needs."

It was no surprise to me that my father could relegate the neighbor's dog to the same corrupt and sad-sounding group of the world's worst leaders. Still, I felt bad for bringing it up, especially at the precise moment that we came upon Riley's white picket fence. Seeing her friend, Riley quickly retrieved as many tennis balls as she could fit in her mouth (amazingly, three) and dropped them at little Krishu's feet. It was almost as if I had staged the whole thing. A wide grin spread across Krishu's face as he picked up the first saliva-slicked ball, reeled his shoulder back, and thrust the ball forward. The moment it left his hand, Riley lunged and charged off, plowing through dirt and leaves to catch the ball before it had even rolled but ten or fifteen feet. Racing back with it clenched in her mouth, panting and drooling, she dropped the ball again at Krishu's feet ready to do it all over again.

As he always does, Krishu reacted with great delight, clapping his hands, almost dancing in place, and laughing loudly. He glanced at both my father and me with his enveloping smile.

"Dada, do it," Krishu ordered. Papa did a double take, looking from Krishu to me and down at the soaked tennis ball. Well aware that a moment before he had likened the game of fetch to the decay of human civilization, he was clearly unsure how to react.

"Dada, do it!!!" Krishu pleaded, his glee poised to take a dramatic turn.

"I'd do it if I were you," I urged my father. I knew how this could turn out.

Papa bent down, plastered a fake smile on his face, and threw the sopping ball a considerable ways farther than Krishu had. Riley was up for it and charged hard through the garden again, catching the ball before it came to a stop. Spinning around on her hind legs, Riley once again rushed back to us with the ball in her mouth.

"Wow!" Krishu stared at his dada in wide-eyed awe. "Dada throw fetch far!!!" At that moment, Krishu's admiration for his grandfather knew no bounds. Sensing this, Dada's smile transformed and was authentic for the first time all day. He needed no prompting now, reaching down to clutch the ball and hurling it even farther this time for Riley to dutifully chase after.

More elation for Krishu. More thrill for Dada. More fetch for Riley. We stood there for ten minutes while Dada impressed Krishu with his arm until, ironically, it was me—Krishu's papa—who had to inform my papa that we had to stop the game and get home.

"But what about Krishu?" Papa asked, concerned.

"Tell him we'll come back tomorrow and play again," I said. "He'll understand."

Hesitantly Papa complied. Initially disappointed, Krishu indeed understood. He knew this routine pretty well. Soon he was running up to the next neighbor's house, where their five-year-old's Tonka trucks were waiting on their doorstep to be admired.

"So," I asked my father, "still so down on fetch?"

He smiled back at me. "I suppose I was wrong." A rare admission, I can tell you. He thought for a moment. "What we just witnessed is playfulness and innocence at its best—from both Krishu and Riley."

"And you, I might add."

"And me." He nodded. "Play behavior in all animals, notably dogs, is a sign of well-being. There is no fear, anger, or sadness in a state of play." He gained momentum. "In the brain, play induces a sensation of pure joy, which in turn produces powerful hormones and chemicals that can have a profound and healthy effect on the body." Papa reminded me that this was all research he'd done years ago while a practicing endocrinologist. (Eat that, Wikipedia!)

"Neurotransmitters like serotonin, dopamine, oxytocin, and naturally induced opiates are antidepressants. They increase self-esteem, happiness, and pleasure—there is a veritable pharmacy organically occurring in your body that makes you healthy if triggered appropriately."

Enter his sweet spot: "All mammals, including humans, are born with a sense of play, but ours tends to fade as we mature into adulthood and take on the burdens of work and responsibility. We'd all be better off if we never stopped playing with ourselves."

Should I? Really, should I? We were having an adult conversation and I knew I should hold the line. I did.

It's true: Dogs innately understand not just the desire for play, but also the need for it. Riley will bring you a ball and lay it at your feet to instigate a game of fetch, or she may send the message more assertively by dropping the ball directly in your hand and then nudging it with her nose. It is beneficial to both your well-being and the dog's—and most certainly Krishu's—to oblige.

Cleo may not be so good at fetch, but she is the ultimate adventurer. No walk around the block with her is complete without at least one hundred stops along the way. A sniff here, a lick there, or her yanking her leash in an attempt to get off the sidewalk when she's spied something that intrigues her.

Now that my dad was in the mood, he noted this. "Curiosity itself is a great example of playfulness and what a profound effect it can have, even physiologically. Cleo's act of sniffing things is not just the embodiment of her curiosity, but it also actually stimulates the pleasure center inside her brain." Cue the oxytocin.

Instinctively I gave Cleo's leash a little more slack. Papa continued: "There's a lot of research that suggests that humans who expose themselves to new things throughout their lives have higher concentrations of the chemicals and hormones I listed, and tend to live more fulfilling and even longer lives."

If you have a dog, then you already understand the vital need for touch for their emotional well-being. It is not an accident that you show your love for your dog by petting her. Her desire to be touched is even stronger than your desire to bury your hands in her warm fur. The head pats and ear scratches are essential to dogs. At the same time, petting a dog creates a sense of calm in people. The difference is that most people are not necessarily conscious of the pleasure they are experiencing, while dogs most certainly are. Ever notice how a dog will at times forcefully shove its head beneath a human hand, seeking touch?

It's in our nature too to experience joy, my dad has reminded me on many occasions, but we let the challenges of modern life muffle this experience. But if you listen, you'll see your best friend is trying to bring this back for you through her own desire for it. Pretty remarkable and intuitive.

We had reached the end of our adventure around the block, coming upon our doorstep. Both Cleo and Krishu did their best to prolong the journey, Krishu urging the one whom he now identified as a weak link—his grandfather—with gestures and a repetitive "fetch . . . fetch . . . fetch . . ." Meanwhile Cleo was pulling on her leash away from the house, obviously seeking more pleasure hunting in the fantasia that was our neighborhood.

Again my father looked at me for guidance. I shook my head, knowing that it was dinnertime for Krishu, to be followed by his bath time, and then the nightly rituals that included reading books, listening to music, good night kisses to Mama, Papa, Dada, and Cleo, and then sleep. There are indeed some important routines and rituals to life.

Candice opened the front door with a big smile on her face. Every single time she looks upon her son, she reacts with instinctive bliss, the same way Krishu does when he plays fetch with Riley, or Cleo reacts when she sees Candice. "Did you have fun on your walk, Krishu?" Candice asked Krishu, sweeping him up into her arms and tickling him.

He nodded excitedly, eager to share. "Dada throw fetch far!!!"

Candice looked at my father, smiling. "He got you to play fetch?" Candice nodded, impressed—she knows my father well enough to understand the significance of the event.

He reciprocated with a smile and his own nod. "Now if only we could teach all the leaders of the world to play fetch, I think we'd be onto something."

LATER THAT EVENING, after Krishu had successfully been put to sleep, Cleo tucked snugly beside him, I drifted back into the living room, finding my father once more staring into his computer.

"More Wikipedia?" I asked.

"Twitter," he answered.

Deepak Chopra is a master tweeter. The man has more to say than anyone in the world. His publishers are no match for him and can hardly keep up with his output. The invention of online platforms, blogs, and social networks where there are no gatekeepers between a man and his audience has been the ultimate gift for my father. He is in constant communication with his audience via his laptop.

"You know, I was thinking," I started, then paused so as to make it seem like I had just casually been thinking and not really scripted the following words. "Maybe we should do this again?"

"Do what?" Papa looked up at me.

"Get together." I shrugged my shoulder involuntarily. "And talk." I nodded, reinforcing what I just said. "I think it's good for Krishu, you know?"

"Okay," he said, unmoved.

"Candice and I are going with Krishu to New York next week for a friend's wedding. You're going to be there, right?"

He nodded, and as if on cue, Cleo sauntered into the living room staring up at each of us, evaluating the playing field. She has an acute sense of the house and anytime she senses that someone is up to something, she finds her way to them to investigate what's going down.

"Listen, Gotham," my father started, sensing something in the silence just like Cleo, "parenting is not easy. Despite the many books on it, including my own"—he smiled at the irony—"there's no perfect method to it, no user manual that guarantees success."

He was quiet for a moment. Cleo drifted his way and lingered again at his feet, identifying the spot where she would come in for her soft landing.

"How do you raise Krishu to be a free thinker, to dream on how to change the world, to be playful and innocent like Cleo and Riley, in a world that demands the opposite, that pushes for rigidity and acquiescence to rules?"

Oh, how I wish Papa had the simple answer and wasn't instead asking a rhetorical question.

"Maybe that's what we should be talking about when we meet again?"

I nodded, knowing my mother would be happy with this development.

Cleo circled her spot at my father's feet and plopped down beneath him. He eyed her dubiously again, not sure what, exactly, she wanted out of him.

three

Papa, do you think being a vegetarian makes you more spiritual?

Are you asking me if I'm vegetarian? I've dabbled with vegetarianism off and on. At this moment I'm a strict vegetarian.

I already knew that. It's not what I'm asking.

Okay, good. What I would say is this: If you want to be healthy, which is a prerequisite for most spiritual experience—because if your body is healthy, your mind is healthy and you can have clarity—vegetarian diets are more conducive to the classic spiritual experience. But if you are changing your diet simply because you want to be spiritual, then the stress that will likely come with changing your diet actually will do the opposite.

What I am saying is that a change in consciousness will bring about a change in behavior and not the other way around. That's the case with most things in life. Until there is a switch in your consciousness, every diet or behavior modification technique is a little more than a fleeting fad.

With all of that said, I think there's a much bigger question lurking here that should be addressed. What does it really mean to be "spiritual"? In our culture we've aligned that with the notion of being vegetarian, good at yoga, and not swearing. But spirituality and the pursuit of it is far beyond that. It is truly the pursuit of higher consciousness and an understanding of the true nature of the cosmos. To reduce spirituality to what your diet is, is to take Einstein's insights in physics and simply say he was good at math.

CLEO IS A PRETTY SEASONED TRAVELER. I OFTEN WISH I'D kept a log all these years, but my guess is she's likely racked up in excess of 100,000 miles, commuting back and forth between NYC and LA, as well as side trips to Atlanta, where Candice's family lives. Since she only weighs about ten pounds, Cleo is allowed to travel "in cabin" with us. She fits quite snugly into her deluxe Sherpa pet carrier, which slides easily beneath the seat in front during takeoff and landing.

We've got our routine down pat—a routine that relies on moving as seamlessly as possible through airport security, ensuring that we're all properly hydrated, and feeding Cleo's drug habit. Cleo's always been a bit of a nervous dog. She hoards food and becomes easily agitated. Occasionally she has trouble sleeping and can spend hours walking in circles around the house. During these periods, she often becomes preoccupied with certain spots in the house that she'll get attached to. She'll crouch behind a door or curl beneath a piece of furniture as if a poltergeist is roaming our grounds. Candice and I like to assign blame for these attributes elsewhere, citing the fact that Cleo is a rescue. Whatever emotional and psychological scars she bore were not on our watch. We've been nothing but loving, if not enabling, parents. We also figure that, as a puppy, Cleo built some sort of intolerance toward men when Candice was in medical school and had only female roommates. It's a questionable theory, but it might explain why Cleo goes absolutely berserk around men she can't identify. It's this attribute more than any of her other eccentricities that generally guarantees disaster when we bring Cleo into public places like airports. Or airplane cabins, for that matter. Or malls, shops, parks, playgrounds, neighbors' homes, banks, or dry cleaners, while we're at it.

Which leads us back to the drugs. Cleo's fix is benzodiazepine, an antianxiety drug that induces drowsiness and sleep. We generally feed Cleo her drugs just as we board the plane so that the first wave of drowsiness kicks in when takeoff is imminent and the rumble and swoop of the plane provokes anxiety not just for dogs, but for humans as well. I can say somewhat sheepishly that the drugs had worked like a charm. We'd never had an incident. Then again, we had never traveled with Cleo and Krishu together until that May trip to New York City. (What we now refer to as that *fateful* trip.)

Krishu is a classic firstborn, the center of his parents' universe. We do *everything* together. We're *that* family. In the year and a half that he's been alive, Krishu has never slept away from either of his parents—not once. I'm not talking about weekends away. I'm talking about separate rooms. We're "cosleepers." There, I said it. It's a term that's often shunned by more progressive parents, especially in those heated debates that take place in the confines of "mommy support groups" and parochial parenting workshops. But I can assure you it's a Western thing. In Santa Monica, cosleeping is a hippie technique. In India, it's just the way it goes.

The same way some of Candice's mommy buddies scowled when Candice let slip our cosleeping arrangement, Nana shook his head dismissively when Candice informed him that, in America, many newborns sleep in their own rooms, away from their parents.

"And sometimes with night nurses," she added, a term that required clarification.

"That explains why there are so many drug addicts in America," Nana declared, a conclusion to which he often returned.

Whatever the case, the fact is that we are just as attached to our little man as he is to us. We also take great comfort in those studies (no doubt conducted by hippie scientists) that conclude that co-sleeping leads to higher immunological benefits, a decreased risk of Sudden Infant Death Syndrome, higher self-esteem, less anxiety, and a litany more of enabling-sounding advantages.

It's not just sleep. Krishu is involved in pretty much every aspect of our lives. He sits with us as we get ready in the morning, comes with us when we take Cleo for her morning walk (she wears two leashes in this case so he can play along), and helps give Cleo her treats.

"Sit, Cleo!" Krishu will demand. And then he'll hurl the treat at her, aiming directly for her snout.

As a responsible parent, a role that's come to me in fits and staggers, I know enough not to directly involve Krishu in Cleo's pill pushing. Nevertheless, as a former kid, I also know the intense attraction of anything forbidden. Kirshu is no different, especially when it comes to Cleo. From her flea medication to her heartworm medication to the other supplements Candice has Cleo downing in her old age, Krishu needs to be in on the action. "Giving medicine" to Cleo is something that is very important to Krishu. It's a way of showing love for the dog. To that extent, I'll usually allow him to hold on to my wrist when giving Cleo her medication. Krishu knows not to touch, and he knows the difference between a pill and a treat.

So it was on that May flight (see also: that *fateful* trip) that Krishu insisted he "help" give Cleo her benzos. *Sure,* I thought.

Why not? So what if I had custody of the dog and the kid? Candice was only as far as the nearest lavatory. What could possibly go wrong?

Plenty, as it turns out.

I held the tiny pill in my hand as Krishu guided my wrist and ordered Cleo to sit. No sweat. Everything was moving along just swell. Traveling with a kid and a dog? I don't know what all the fuss is about. But right at the moment when we were about to administer the pill, a flight attendant strolled by to make sure we were wearing our seat belts. Instinctively I attempted to clasp my hand, while Krishu for some reason jerked it forward. The effect was similar to that of a slingshot, with a benzo instead of a rock. Little Krishu being no Goliath, the tiny pill soared over Cleo's head beneath the dark confines of the seat in front of us. Cleo spied the shadows beneath and then turned back to me with a look that was both helpless and hapless. Clearly the mere thought of her chasing the pill was beneath her.

Of course, as the big papa of this household—and someone who knew his wife wouldn't be thrilled with the way things were playing out—I got on my hands and knees and started the search. That's where Candice found me when she returned from the lavatory—with Krishu giddily climbing all over my back and Cleo licking my face.

"What's wrong?" she asked.

"Um, nothing." I leaped up instinctively. "Krishu threw a Matchbox car down there and I was just looking for it."

"Did you find it?" Candice asked innocently.

"Nope," I answered, empty-handed. "It must have rolled down."

She shrugged. "Did you give Cleo her meds?"

I nodded vigorously, shoving Cleo's head down into the bag and zipping it shut, while locking eyes with Krishu as if to send a message. His limited vocabulary and blind trust in his father could be counted on, I judged instinctively.

Soon the pilot came on overhead and previewed the flight path, duration, and assorted details. As the plane rolled out toward the runway and the attendants went over safety instructions and Candice unveiled the first of many distractions for Krishu (coloring books, stickers, puzzles, etc.), I eyed Cleo, who seemed peacefully at ease in her bag. Pleased with myself and my simple cover-up, I dared to think that maybe we were way too paranoid about Cleo and needed to lay off enabling her habit. We might show a little more faith in her, I thought to myself; trust her ability to control her own moods without the aid of powerful narcotics. These are the types of instincts parents should nurture.

I should have known better.

As soon as the plane rumbled down the runway, picking up thrust toward takeoff, a whimper emerged from Cleo's bag. No big deal, I thought to myself. Even under the aid of her drugs, Cleo occasionally reacted with soft agitated cries, especially during takeoff and the moments afterward when her ears popped. This was no different. It didn't even register with Candice, who, with Krishu, remained focused on Dora and Diego. But then another groan emerged from the bag, this one far stronger than the first. Candice glanced downward and then toward me.

"Is she okay?"

"Yeah, she's fine." I nodded reassuringly. "Rough takeoff," I added as the plane soared gracefully into the air.

But Cleo was anything but fine. And she quickly made us aware of it with a very audible yelp this time. Now not just Candice but the couple across the aisle stared over at us suspiciously.

"That's strange," I said, putting my hand on her bag, determined at this stage to keep my ill-conceived charade going. This time as the plane veered hard, making its turn after lifting off over the Pacific and heading back east, Cleo let loose with a rapid fire of agonized cries. As if she had a deep sense of foreboding for some imminent danger, she culminated her cry with a soulful, boisterous groan.

Passengers all around us clued into the awkward sounds coming from our aisle. I shrugged my shoulders and smiled.

"Pick her up," Candice urged me, sensing the same heat.

I followed her orders and lifted Cleo's bag onto my lap, staring into the mesh, trying to calm Cleo with soothing words and sounds. But she'd have none of it. She started to claw at the fabric frantically with her tiny paws. Her eyes wide, pupils fully dilated, this was a dog on the edge, a canine junkie that needed her fix.

"Take it easy, Cleo." I fumbled with the zipper on the side of the bag and pulled out the prescription bottle for the medicine. I cracked it open and my own eyes widened with panic when I saw it was empty.

"What are you doing?" Candice inquired.

"Don't you see?" I answered. "She needs more drugs!" I calmed myself and took on more of a solemn tone. "She's built up a tolerance to this stuff."

"Well, there aren't any more pills. You already gave her the last one." God bless Candice for never doubting me. Krishu started to cry, Cleo's anxiety affecting him. "Calm her down," Candice ordered.

Determined to make my cover-up succeed, I unzipped the top of Cleo's bag and stuck my hand inside to stroke her. Cleo, seizing the moment, climbed right over my palm and leaped out of the bag. I tried to wrangle her but she wriggled free and pounced away from me, landing on Krishu, whose expression transformed from abject terror to absolute glee, as if he had just witnessed a fellow comrade sprung from death row.

Free at last, Cleo made for the hills, or at least for the center aisle. Mouths agape, Candice and I watched as Cleo landed in the middle of the aisle and reared back on her hind legs, barking raucously, before tearing off full tilt toward the front of the plane.

"Holy shit," I exclaimed.

Krishu turned to me, his grin widening ever more. He knew this taboo word that was used far too often for his mother's liking. "Sheeeet!!!!"

The whole cabin was flustered now as the other passengers registered what was happening. I leaped into the aisle and searched for Cleo. She had made it about twelve rows forward, where once more she stood poised, weight on her hind legs, barking full pitch at a terrified young man who reared back in his seat. I rushed off after her as the flight attendants wrestled out of their jump seats to join in the fray.

Over the next ten minutes, I gave chase, dodging and weaving my way through the cabin along with three decidedly irritated flight attendants. For Cleo, it had quickly turned into a joyous game. As soon as one of us would close in on her, she'd elude capture, sliding beneath a seat or leaping straight over frenzied passengers. At first I too was frantic, but in Cleo I could see a switch had occurred. Her initial panic had transformed into playfulness. It was all a game to her now. I could only attribute the passengers' alarm to the fact that we were all locked into a confined space as we steadily made our way through fifteen thousand feet. Cleo—at her most ferocious—could barely subdue an insect, a gladiatorial combat we witnessed occasionally in our backyard.

At long last, a woman in seat 7C managed to soothe Cleo by

offering her a piece of a fresh croissant she had brought onto the plane. Ever the well-behaved dog when it came to exotic French pastry, Cleo calmed down as the woman skillfully fed her and then held her in her arms until I arrived.

"Thank you so much." I took Cleo from her as Cleo wrestled me to make sure the croissant came with us. "I owe you a croissant." I shrugged sheepishly.

"Buy me a cocktail instead." She smiled back.

I marched back to our row, avoiding the glares of our fellow passengers, and plopped down beside Candice and Krishu.

"You didn't give her her drugs, did you?" Candice shook her head at me, disappointment all over her face.

"Sheeeet!!!" Krishu reaffirmed.

My thoughts exactly.

FLYING FROM THE WEST to East Coast you essentially lose the day. If you leave Los Angeles around breakfast time, you barely make it to New York in time for dinner. Add the fact that we remain in "orange alert," and you can't bring aboard so much as a bottle of water. And because nowadays you can't get a peanut on a commercial airline for anything short of a ten-spot, flying across the country is like fasting for Ramadan. While I am willing to shell out the big bucks for my son, I'm patently averse to enabling the airlines by buying and eating their pressurized food. The consequence, of course, is that upon landing in NYC, I'm always famished. Still, no matter my desperation, even I realize that my needs are no longer a priority in our little family. First comes Krishu— changing the diaper, making sure his clothes are dry, that he's outfitted right so as to neither be too hot nor too cold, ensuring that he's not hungry, thirsty, tired, or otherwise off-kilter. Next in line is Cleo, ensuring her food and water are out, that she's warm and has a place to sleep, and that she's had a chance to walk around the block, shake off the effects of the flight, and do her business. This night, by the time we blazed through all of these required rituals, it was past ten p.m. and my hunger knew no bounds. Realizing that our options were dwindling quickly, I became frantic, nervous that I'd have to resort to stale pizza or the suspiciously shiny food that sits beneath heat lamps all day at the closest corner deli.

"What's wrong with that food?" Papa shrugged.

"Nothing." I shrugged too, not wanting to get into it. "There has to be something else in the neighborhood that's open and good."

Papa raised his eyebrows mischievously. "I know just the place."

His clock thrown off by the transcontinental voyage, and now excited by the city lights and the surprise appearance of his dada amid it all, Krishu was equally excited by the prospects of our dinner adventure. "We go," he sang, clutching his grandfather's sleeve as we left the apartment.

We were escorted by my father to the most unlikely of places just a few blocks away—an old New York City landmark named Rosie O'Grady's. What made it an unlikely destination for the Chopra family is that Rosie O'Grady's is most well known for its chops, and the Chopras—notably Deepak—are not. When I raised this conundrum with my father, he got a little defensive. "They have grilled asparagus," he said.

The truth is, it's not easy being Deepak Chopra. He's unlike other celebrities in the sense that he's not some A-list actor or filmmaker. He's not an NFL superstar who packs stadiums, not a rock star who rocks sold-out shows. Those sorts of stars have colleagues. For every Madonna, there's a Beyoncé. For every Cruise, there's a Pitt, every Kobe, a LeBron. But there's only one Deepak. In our world of celebrity obsession, where every move by a famous person is tweeted, paparazzi stalked, and Perez-ed out, Deepak's pretty much one of a kind.

And then there's what he's famous for, a holiness of sorts. Many of his fans and followers believe he sweats wisdom, breathes spiritual affirmations, and can do no wrong. And while he's never outwardly declared that he's a practitioner of things like yoga or veganism, most are convinced of it. The fact is that Papa's not very hard-core about anything in life. "A rigid life is a static life," he likes to say. For the record, he's an exercise fanatic (more elliptical than downward dog) and not big on steaks and chops.

Still, he's particularly mindful not to shatter the illusion. In his mind, it's good for people to have certain ideals, if even he has to bear the burden of representing them. So while he's not one to shy away from a steakhouse when his family is hungry, you won't find us sitting in the front of the dining room.

"The usual spot, Doc?" the gray-haired maître d' asked as we stepped into the restaurant. Papa nodded and we followed the man through the boisterous place. A cluster of young bankers stood by the worn bar, trading barbs with hoarse voices. At its end, both the bartender and another suit cringed as they stared up at the TV hanging in the corner, seeing the Yankees squander another game as part of their early season malaise. A young woman texted away furiously on her BlackBerry as her date stirred his drink with a straw. Leaving the bar area, we strode through the spacious and busy dining room toward the back of the restaurant.

"A bottle of Perrier, Doc?" the maître d' inquired as we took our seats. My father nodded. Gray Hair flashed a smile and disappeared.

"Come here often, Papa?" Candice grinned at my father.

"Rumi," Papa replied, invoking his favorite poet, "says, 'Judge

me, define me, put me in a box and that box will be your coffin.'"
He smiled back at her and donned his "Liberace glasses," as I like
to call them. They're bright sparkly red and have become quite
iconic among both his fans and the conservative critics who stalk
and publicly critique his every aphorism.

Staring at the menu, he remarked, "I hear they're famous for
their steaks."

For what it's worth, on this night, Candice and I were the only
ones ordering massive steaks bedecked with sides. While Papa may
be conscious and concerned with appearances in situations like
these, Candice and I certainly were not. We were hungry, and our
hunger won out.

No matter his parents' ravenous state, and no matter how fine
an establishment a place like Rosie O'Grady's might be, Krishu will
generally lose his patience within five minutes. The great irony is
that in a less refined place, he can seemingly last for hours. Give
him a few dumplings, chopsticks, and some soy sauce to play with
at a rundown Chinese restaurant and he's as quiet as a fifty-year-
old suit at the Four Seasons. Take him anywhere with a tablecloth
and bring on the jihad. Apropos, tonight's distraction of an array of
wineglasses, cutlery, and a salt shaker shaped like a swan stretched
him about six minutes. It was time for a diversion. Papa, seeing that
Candice and I were weary from our long day of traveling, volun-
teered to take Krishu for a look-see around the bustling restaurant.
With gasps of delight and words soaked in anticipation—"Does
Krishu want to see taxis?"—my son can be goaded into almost anything. We've all learned this, and my father has, not surprisingly,
become a master.

In the brief time that we have had Krishu and Cleo together,
Candice and I have learned to value any moment we are without
both of them. We've become adept at quickly downing meals,

showering in thirty-second intervals, sleeping for mere minutes, engaging in conversations that rely on elevator pitches, and making critical decisions based purely on instinct. At that moment, however, sitting there with bottles of cabernet and Perrier between us, and nothing pressing to do, we breathed.

"What should we do with Cleo tomorrow?" I broke the silence.

"During the wedding?" Candice sipped her wine, drawing from it as much pleasure as possible.

I nodded. Since the wedding was in Jersey, bookended before and after various rituals, we were likely to be gone from morning to night.

She shrugged. "We'll leave her with Papa."

Candice is not a shrugger. Unless it involved a pair of shoes on sale at Bloomingdale's or *Us Weekly* at the supermarket counter, she was also not an impulsive decision-maker. She had thought about this.

"You really think we can leave Cleo with my father for the whole day?" I calculated the odds as to which one of them would want to jump out of the sixty-ninth-story window first.

"He did play some part in raising you, you know?" She nodded.

"I don't know." I shook my head, unwilling to be swayed by my own existence.

"Look." She pointed toward the large window in the big dining room. Through it we could see Krishu on Papa's shoulders as my father pointed to yellow taxicabs and big blue buses racing down Seventh Avenue. "You and your sister didn't think he would be much of a grandfather, but he's figuring it out."

"Yeah, but," I countered, "he's not a dog person."

"Neither is she," Candice argued.

"That doesn't make any sense." I shook my head.

"They'll be fine. Trust me."

Between Candice and me, *trust* is kind of a golden word. She doesn't use it lightly and when she asks for it, she expects it. It's one of my wife's greatest qualities. Since the day I met her my freshman year of college, she's been my best friend and constant companion. Even as we made our way through, at times struggling, a decade's worth of individual and collective growth, from teenagers through almost our entire twenties before we tied the knot, her commitment to our bond has been the single point of stability through it all.

"Okay." I took a swig of my wine.

Silence.

"Wow, can you hear that?" Candice asked.

"No." I smiled. "And it's fabulous."

Sure, the overaged frat boys at the bar were arguing more heatedly, the bartender and others were cheering loudly at the Yankees' inevitable comeback, but there was no crying, no toddler demanding this or that, no dog barking furiously. We might as well have been in a seminary tucked away in the French Alps. At night. During a snowstorm.

"Do you think they're okay?" Candice couldn't resist.

Before I could even answer, Krishu's wails became audible. A moment later Papa arrived back at the table with a crying Krishu in his arms.

"What happened?" I asked as I rose from my seat to take the baton that was my sweet crying boy.

"I don't know." My father shook his head. "We were fine. I was showing him the big *moo cow* in the entryway."

We had all noted the massive ceramic cow in the front of the restaurant. It was one of many art pieces spread across the city, porcelain-like bovines painted with assorted designs. Surely it felt a bit strange for one of them to be placed in the entryway of a restaurant that was most well known for the slaughtering of cows and overpricing their garlic-soaked grilled flanks. Then again, we hadn't been swayed.

"And then I showed him the moo cows coming out of the kitchen," Papa added.

This is what we meant when Mallika and I expressed concern for my father's grandfatherly role. For all the revelations on higher consciousness that he comes up with almost daily, the simple things sometimes elude him.

"What?" He stared at us blankly as both Candice and I shook our heads and Krishu wailed even more loudly.

"Moo cow no eat!" he screamed.

And then like the crescendo of the Boston Pops, everything culminated at once. Krishu's cries quickly grew louder as Papa rationalized how this was a moment for us to explain to Krishu how all of life was constantly recycling itself. "We too are nothing more than wisps of matter that will be digested through the planet like that steak will be through you."

"Moo cow no eat!!!!"

"I'll take him," Candice said, reaching for Krishu just as the waiters arrived with our sizzling steaks.

"MOO COW NO EAT!!!!!"

"Papa—let's switch places," Candice said as she slid out from the couch. "Just go ahead and put the plates down," she instructed the waiters even as she rose from her seat. Her wizardry and reorganizing everything on the fly is something to admire.

"Where should I sit?" Papa asked just as his sizzling asparagus arrived.

"Right there." She pointed where her steak sat waiting. "Just rearrange the plates."

"Moo cow no eat, Mama," Krishu cried unrelentingly as my

father slid into his seat and I settled into mine, determined at long last to get to my meal.

All of a sudden a giddy voice rang out. "Oh my God." We all looked up to find a fifty-ish white woman standing in front of our table. Her eyes were wide with exhilaration. "You're the writer Deepak Chopra!" she said excitedly.

"I am," my father said graciously.

"Wow, this is so amazing!" She fumbled through her purse and pulled out a camera phone.

"I've read like every one of your books. My favorite is that one *The Seven Spiritual Laws of Success.*"

Papa smiled back at her pleasantly, thanking her.

"I totally get it. We all practice the Law of Pure Potentiality in my office every Monday." She nodded. "When you know all living things are connected, then you appreciate the world in a whole different way."

She stood proudly, her smile beaming down at all of us. And then as she took in the massive chop and goblet of wine sitting right in front of Papa, that expression of unmitigated joy transformed to one of absolute terror.

Following her expression, he seemed to register what she was thinking and started to stammer through an explanation.

But she cut him off. "What the hell are you eating?"

"MOM CALLED," PAPA remarked as we walked Cleo around the block after dinner. Candice and I had inhaled our food, washed it down with our beverages, skipped right over dessert and coffee, left a generous tip because of the profound mess our son had made under the table, and rushed home before Krishu's total and complete meltdown. As Candice now dashed through his nighttime rituals, I played my part of taking Cleo around the block. It's a routine I quite enjoy. No matter where we might be, the last thing I do before heading off to sleep is take Cleo for a walk. There's a certain nostalgia to doing so in New York City, where Cleo spent the first four years of her life. Despite the fact that she's now lived in sunny Santa Monica for just over seven years, we still like to think of her as a "city dog." *Tough* will never be a quality that Cleo will be defined by, but resilient and lively and feisty—just like New York City—certainly would be.

Even as we emerged from the elevator onto the street, Cleo's step seemed to take on an added spring. The smells of the city—especially down at her level—seemed to energize her. A New York City street at night, with its piles of garbage leaking out unidentifiable fluids, food discarded by restaurants closed for the night, other city dogs' markings, and the occasional homeless person who has found his spot for the night make for a cornucopia of splendors Cleo could spend hours investigating. If given the chance, she'd spend all night on this block. And there's a part of me, enjoying watching her in such bliss, that would be happy to do it with her.

"Nana's condition has stabilized." He nodded. "They'll probably keep him in the hospital for a few days and then let Mom bring him home."

"Great." I stopped to let Cleo sniff out something beside a newspaper dispenser. "So does that mean Mom will come back soon?"

"No." Papa shook his head. "Nana's going to have to take it easy for a few weeks, even months. He cannot stress his heart. Mom needs to be there to keep everyone calm."

It's my mother's greatest gift. Her presence brings that sense of calmness to everyone around her. No matter the storm brewing, whether it's a sickness in the family, the stress of a grandchild's first day of school, or just the mundane anxieties of a normal day, my mom has a way of gracefully putting people at ease. All of us—my father, Mallika, and me, and even our respective spouses and children now—have become increasingly dependent on her as the years passed.

But most of all, my father's emotional dependence on my mother has become clear the last few years. Even now, over sixty, he spends most of the year on the road hustling from one side of the planet to the other. One day he's in Chicago, the next he's in London. The following day he's in Amsterdam and then he's in Tokyo. It's an absolute whirlwind that never stops. Every few weeks when it lets up for a few days, he lands in NYC or LA and my mom is almost always there to receive him, to help him unpack and repack, to make a home-cooked meal just the way he likes it, to go see a movie or a show together, or just go for early morning walks in Central Park. Their relationship has a throwback quality to it that is almost impossible to come across in our more modern times. It's not so fashionable these days to use the phrase "Behind every good man is a great woman" or to assign traditional gender roles to men and women. It's a violation of the cultural progress we claim to have made in our society and an absolute taboo to talk about the idea that a husband and wife may play those traditional roles.

When I look at my parents, though, they seem to have transcended those taboos. Their relationship—undoubtedly not without its own continued peaks and valleys, pressure points and anxieties—is rooted in something special that evolves only after significant time, having been nurtured by attention, respect, and empathy for each other.

What is that special ingredient that makes relationships last and grow stronger over time? What evolves them from partnerships to bonds, from social contracts to spiritual unions? And not just between a husband and wife, but between friends, siblings, parents and their children?

"Companionship," my father declares as we come to a final stop at the side of the building where clearly another dog has just been, having left its mark maybe moments before. "In one word, it's companionship."

It's a word pregnant with meaning and context. It intimates friendship and trust and loyalty and intimacy.

But alas, that's as far as we'll get tonight. We've made it around the block by now and it's time to go upstairs and off to sleep.

CANDICE AND I had already been seeing each other for over four years—all through our undergraduate years at Columbia University—when she called me in the fall of 1998 to say that she was in New Jersey and was contemplating purchasing a cute little rescue puppy that she was holding in her hands.

I was unsure how to respond, instinctively sensing it was a bad idea. Candice was a second-year medical school student still at Columbia University, situated way uptown in a part of the city known affectionately as Dominican Harlem. I had moved out to Los Angeles, where I was working. We had mutually expressed our continued commitment to each other and willingness to try out the long-distance thing. My job as an international news correspondent took me to far-off places like Chechnya and Sri Lanka, Seoul and Bogotá, to cover stories and conflicts that often slipped out of the headline news. Our broadcast was targeted at teenagers who didn't have much context for the stories or places we were covering, and as a result I'd spend days or even weeks in some exotic city or war zone before logging the long trip back to the States. As often as I could I'd make pit stops in New York City, where

I'd crash out at Candice's dorm and hang around to spend time with her in the brief hours her hectic med school schedule permitted.

For me, it was an ideal situation. I knew Candice was special. She balanced me in a way that felt right. While I had barely graduated from college, earning my last credit the day before graduation (by getting a five-point independent study credit) courtesy of my parents paying full-freight admission for four years, Candice had double majored, earned enough credits to graduate in three years, and had done so while working part-time to get a head start on paying off the considerable student loans she had taken to earn her degree.

Even after graduating, while I used my news reporter job as an excuse to gallivant across the globe, hanging out with the likes of Jihadis and narco-traffickers, weapons dealers and motley gangsters, Candice was fixed on getting a medical degree and entering the world of medicine. Where I was fundamentally incapable of thinking through what I really wanted out of life, she seemed to have been born with a sixth sense that told her exactly what she wanted. As we had started dating when we were essentially still kids—both of us eighteen years old at the time—and managed to stay together all through college and now into life after school, we knew each other in a way that no one else, even in our families, did.

That's partly the reason my mind raced ahead. Assembling the facts together as I knew them. Candice was already beyond the point of "thinking about getting a new dog." She had already made the decision and was now orchestrating things to make it so.

"Okay . . ." I said hesitantly, carefully feeling out the murkiness between us. One wrong sigh, a subtle turn in tone, let alone saying something stupid, could result in catastrophe and a horribly high phone bill.

"Don't worry, I'm not expecting you to do anything," she said sharply.

Incredible, I thought. She had smelled out my anxiety before I had even identified it.

"It's . . . not that," I stammered. "I just . . ."

It was totally that. I was happy where my relationship was with Candice. Why rock the boat? Why introduce another being into the equation? Even though it had been well over a decade since Nicholas, I remembered what a commitment he was. And now I realized, the real commitment was not going to be to the dog in this case, it was going to be to each other.

"What do you think?" Candice asked.

"What do you want me to say?" I offered, saying the exact wrong thing at the wrong time in the wrong tone.

"What is that supposed to mean?" she fired back. "I want you to say whatever you want to say."

No, she didn't. I knew this terrain well. I was quickly becoming Harry Potter, lost in the shadowy woods, with the threat of Lord Voldemort quickly closing in on me. Candice had something she wanted me to say, all right, but she wanted me to say it without her prodding and prompting me. Even worse, she wanted me to *mean it.*

But it was too late for me. "What kind of dog is it?"

A beat.

"She's really cute, Gotham," Candice gushed.

It was as if I had thrown a Hail Mary pass to myself. Steering the conversation to how cute Cleo was, albeit unintentionally, was the first of many times that Cleo would save my ass from certain doom.

"Her mom's a Maltese. Not sure what her dad is. Or who her dad is. Oh my God, Gotham, she's so adorable. She fits in the palm of my hand. She's so tiny!!!!" Candice was rolling now. She was near tears. "So you think I should get her? I should totally get her, shouldn't I?"

"Yeah, sure," I said trying to convince myself. "Definitely . . ."

"Awesome!" she screamed gleefully. "I need you to send a hundred dollars. That's how much she costs and I only have ten dollars in my bank account!"

I often joke with Candice all these years later that Cleo's one-hundred-dollar worth was the most misleading price tag I've ever encountered. For the record, we're still paying off those damned student loans.

"Don't forget," Candice likes to remind me these days, "I'm the mother of your son. That's priceless."

Touché. Truth be told, in her own way, even when I met her for the first time a few weeks after Candice brought her home from Jersey, Cleo too proved to be priceless. In the weeks that had passed, she had grown from the size of a little puffball of fur that fit in the palm of one hand to a slightly larger puffball of fur that fit into both palms placed side by side.

At night—then and now—Cleo likes to curl up beside me when she sleeps, tucking herself usually snugly against my legs or even my chest if I'll indulge her. Candice jokes it's because she likes my smell, which I'm guessing is not a compliment. Early on when I'd linger around Candice's dorm room, waiting for her to get back from class and then shower off the formaldehyde smell she'd earned dissecting human cadavers, Cleo would loyally follow me around wherever I went—from sitting in bed to reading a magazine to watching television in the living room, to sitting in the bathroom reading a magazine—always mindful to ensure that one of her extremities was touching mine. It was an odd trait I'd never really noticed in other dogs. Cleo's need for physical contact was obvious and deliberate. Gradually I became more adventurous with her, taking her on long walks up in the Cloisters and then on the subway downtown, where she'd join me as I ran errands until Candice would again be free.

One afternoon after a long day out in the city, Cleo and I fell asleep on the couch in front of the TV. Candice returned in her medical scrubs (she had been working an ER shift) to find the two of us curled up, keeping each other warm. I woke up to find Candice sitting on the opposite couch, staring at us, an unreadable expression on her face.

"Okay," I said as I lumbered up from the couch, Cleo shifting slightly but not ready herself to get up, "this dog's all right."

Candice started to cry. Quickly her gradual tears turned to big heavy ones. I stared at her, concerned. "What?"

"I witnessed my first death today in the ER," she sobbed.

"Someone you knew?" I asked, concerned.

"No." She shook her head, composing herself. "A family, they had been in a car accident . . ."

The details were considerably worse. A couple with their two young children had gotten into a wreck on the West Side Highway. The mother had been pronounced dead on arrival at the hospital, and the medical team in the ER—of which Candice was a part—was unable to revive one of the little girls. She too had passed away in front of their very eyes.

"I don't think I could ever, ever . . ." Candice started to cry uncontrollably again. "I mean, if you knew that was going to happen to you, I don't think I could even love someone, have children, you know . . . if I knew I was going to lose them."

I took her into my arms and tried to soothe her. "It's okay."

For another hour, Candice cried until she gradually drifted off to sleep. As if sensing her despair, Cleo left my side and wedged herself tightly beside Candice.

From that moment on, I've always believed Cleo has an amazing ability to read those she is close to. In particular when someone she cares for is sad, she expresses her empathy by touching him, spreading her warmth, and making sure that he knows that in her, he has a companion that will stay there for as long as necessary. Likewise, when excitement grips the house, it pulses through Cleo. She runs around the house, barking loudly, skipping in circles. On lazy days, especially when Candice wants to lie around the house, eat breakfast in bed, watch a movie, Cleo can lie still for hours, keeping an eye on her master just in case the mood should change. She's connected to us at some emotional and spiritual level—that I am sure of, and I've never needed any elaborate experiments nor studies to validate it.

I'M NOT BIG into weddings and all that goes into them—the elaborate dress codes, the endless formalities and bizarre rituals, the lame toasts and cheesy bands are all too much for me—so having the built-in excuse of a child, especially one as rambunctious and impatient as Krishu, is a real gift. I often find myself with Krishu hanging outside chapels and reception halls alongside smokers while the strange chicken dances and conga lines ensue inside. The real prize, however, is that when I've reached my tolerance after several hours donated to a wedding, I get to cut out and use my boy as an excuse: "Shoot, would love to stay but he's had a really long day! He's overtired. Don't want him to get unwell . . ." Krishu is great at playing out his role. He cries and wriggles at all the key moments. He's really got spectacular timing, a Brando-esque instinct for playing up the drama at just the right time.

To Candice's great chagrin, I spend most of my time at weddings fixated on how to make sure that my son loses his shit just when I need him to. Admittedly this really undermines any chance that I will appreciate any part of a wedding. Of course, Candice is just the opposite. She loves them—especially the super-melodramatic parts like when the bride walks down the aisle or the couple takes their vows or does their first dance to the tunes of those same cheesy wedding bands. There's a reason, of course. It's these souped-up rituals that really capture what marriages are about—commitment and companionship. A successful marriage is an ongoing commitment to each other and nurtures a growing sense of companionship over time. But those special rituals, so well choreographed in the all-consuming endeavor that is a wedding, are the iconic moments that commemorate them.

At the New Jersey wedding in question, the union of a college friend with his beautiful bride, all the various forces of the universe gloriously aligned. Candice got her fill of dramatic emotional moments—the bride actually went off script at the wedding and confessed to the sadness of her late father not being able to be there—and I got to carry Krishu around looking at the Statue of Liberty through the extended cocktail period. Conveniently, Krishu busted his nut some ten minutes into dinner—just when the lame toasts were beginning. Exit Chopra family.

Add the fact that both Candice and I were acutely aware that my father had been left alone with Cleo (or vice versa) for close to seven hours, and getting out of that wedding we were like Bonnie and Clyde after a heist.

"Do you think Cleo and my dad did okay?" I asked Candice as I held Krishu's sleeping body in my lap as we rode the PATH train back to Manhattan.

"I'm sure they survived." She shrugged.

Basic survival, of course, was not quite what I was hoping for. That I was counting on.

"We have to show confidence in your dad," Candice asserted. "If we are not confident in him, how can he be confident in himself?"

This felt familiar—Candice manufacturing confidence that would translate into self-esteem and empowerment, in this case for my dad. It was nice to know that he was now included in our motley crew.

"Stop worrying," Candice insisted. "They're fine."

There used to be a time when merely inserting the key into the lock drew Cleo's attention. If there were multiple locks to be undone, you would hear her whimpering and clawing at the door.

These days, with her deteriorated hearing, she's not as sharp in her responses. Hence it's my job really to locate Cleo when we get home, lasso her with her leash, and take her for a walk. She tends to doze in a few familiar areas—atop a piece of dirty laundry if she can score it, or on a bed (preferably unmade), or as a last resort, in her own dog bed. My parents' Manhattan apartment, however, was a whole new frontier for Cleo and I had no idea where to look first.

As I lurked around the apartment, I noticed a variety of dog toys spread around the main living room. Newly opened plush toys, chews, a rubber bone, two pinkish rubbery balls, and a pig's ear lay scattered. Bits of dog food dotted the dark wooden floor. Still no sign of Cleo to go with her obviously new accoutrements. Next up, the kitchen. Another pig's ear lying between two dog bowls—one filled with water and another with milk.

Milk! The move of an amateur. Cleo's digestion is dodgy to say the least.

I made a beeline for my parents' bedroom. Dim city lights poured in through the window, just enough to make out the large pillows scattered across the floor. They'd clearly been tossed from the bed haphazardly to make room for Cleo and my father, who both were in a deep, hard slumber. Predictably Cleo lay curled and tucked against my father's legs. She was the first to stir, hearing me at last.

"Come on, Cleo," I beckoned her, "you want to go for a walk?"

She lumbered up, her tail wagging. Arching her back, she stretched herself out before skipping toward me, her tongue wagging now with equal energy.

Cleo's movements stirred my father. His eyes flashed open.

"You're back?"

I nodded, hooking Cleo's leash to her collar. "Yeah. Looks like you guys had quite a day. Did you give her milk?"

"She asked for it," my father said with a nod, "when I was putting it in my coffee."

There was nothing to say. "Okay—I'm going to take her around the block," I said.

My father nodded again. "I'll go with you."

SUMMER NIGHTS IN New York City are the best. While the days can be sticky and oppressive, a stroll under the stars is unlike anything else. The warm air, the brisk breeze—it makes for the perfect backdrop to walk your dog when you may need a decent runway to make sure her imminent diarrhea arrives before heading back upstairs. Tonight, that runway is Broadway.

"Probably want to avoid milk next time," I noted to my father as we turned the corner onto Broadway.

"She's hard to say no to," he answered. "She wanted pretty much every toy in the store."

"I noticed."

"She's funny, though," he reflected.

"In what way?" Punch line please.

"She's very affectionate. Just followed me around all day. Whatever room I was in, no matter what I was doing. I almost fell over her a few times." He shook his head.

"Are all dogs like that?" Papa looked down at Cleo curiously.

Cleo is indeed a people dog in that way, more than a dog's dog at least. She likes company, especially as it relates to the family. I've never regarded her as particularly needy, but admittedly it's a fine line.

"I don't know," I answered. "Could have been the pig's ears. She loves those things."

"I can't believe they are real!"

I knew exactly where he was coming from. The discovery that pig's ears are really, well, pig's ears, is a frequently disturbing revelation for the amateur dog owner. But Cleo loves them like nothing else.

"I'm sure everyone thinks their dog is unique, but Cleo is definitely one of a kind." I guided her toward the little dirt patch on the sidewalk, hoping we could get this party started. She peed out of obligation but moved on. No dice.

"Her persistence is infectious," he continued. "All of a sudden when she wasn't following me for a minute, I started to worry. I went looking for her."

"Yeah." I nodded, relating. "She's like that."

"That's the thing about all dogs, isn't it? Nicholas, Cleo, when you get them you know exactly how things will mostly play out. You're going to form an intense bond with them, even through no effort of your own. You're going to grow together, play together, and love each other. And then, the dog is going to die." He was silent.

"Dogs are different from humans that way. Even the best of marriages are unpredictable. You don't know what life is going to bring your way. People change, but dogs don't. Not really."

It's hard to argue. Cleo is the classic case study. Since the day

Candice brought her home in the palm of her hand, and even now with age slowing her down, she's remained the same playful, loyal dog with the same idiosyncrasies and deep bond to family.

"So why, then, if the trajectory of the relationship is predictable, and fated to end in emotional pain, do we endure it?" Papa looked down at Cleo.

I shrugged my shoulders. I knew I didn't really have to answer in this case. No matter—Papa is used to answering his own questions. It's the root of his success.

"Because of the companionship. The emotional fulfillment that we draw from the relationship is worth everything else that comes along with it."

Is that really that different from the relationships we form with one another?

It's one of the things I think about often as I watch my son grow every day. What sort of boy will he become? As his personality further evolves and matures, will he and I have things in common? What if we don't? Sometimes at night, I lie awake and stare at him and wonder to myself if I am prepared for the emotional attachment that I have already made to his being, and the increased one I make every day. I think back to that day Candice as a young medical student witnessed a family torn apart by a horrible car accident. Every day bad things happen to good people. Tragedy tears apart families, rips to shreds the deepest connections that we make with one another.

"Fear is a big part of human relationships, or often why we don't fully form them. The fear of emotional pain and suffering, of making yourself vulnerable to someone else, the threat of loss and hurt that can come from that vulnerability.

"Marriages, children, friendships, all the various forms of companionship—they are intrinsically dangerous because we can

never predict where they are going. And yet, we have to go into them with the same willingness, courage, and enthusiasm with which we form our bonds with our dogs."

Cleo set her sights on a pigeon a few feet ahead of us. She yanked her leash toward it. Papa and I followed.

"But the most important things I think we can learn about relationships are from Cleo herself, the bonds that she builds. Her relationships are rooted in loyalty and trust, forgiveness and nonjudgment. She gives affection but she receives it too. That's empowering—to be loved but also to be able to offer it to another being."

Cleo also empathizes no matter your mood. She's willing to play, cry, or just lounge around and listen if that's what you need. Throughout our life with her, almost on a daily basis, we have traversed these peaks and valleys with her.

"She's quite remarkable really," Papa said.

I too looked down at her, seeing her in a new light all of a sudden. Who knew Cleo held the keys to forming perfect relationships? Dr. Phil, watch out.

"What's she doing?" Papa said, his expression turning from admiration to confusion as Cleo squatted.

I shook my head and winced. "Yeah, that's why no matter how much she asks for it, hold out on the milk."

four

*Papa, what would you do if you thought no one would ever find out?
I like to think that's the way I already live. There's a quote from
Rumi: "I want to sing like birds sing, not worrying about who hears and
what they think."*

So is that the way you roll?

*Not really. But your question raises an interesting phenomenon. When
anyone does something that becomes part of the public eye, then the public
creates an image of that person. And then that image, because it never
conforms to the reality of that person, sooner than later it gets defiled. It
happens every time. And when that image is inevitably defiled, society
gets enraged at the person when in fact they should be getting enraged at
themselves for creating the image in the first place.*

*It's a tangled web, for sure. The perfect example is someone like Tiger
Woods. He and all of the people that believed in him cocreated the mythic
persona that he started to become. Not just because he was a dominant
athlete on the golf course (which he presumably wouldn't ever want to
change) but because of everything else—all of the multi-million-dollar
endorsement deals—that he signed onto and the image they perpetuated
together. He didn't need to create that image that he allowed people to
make of him but he did, probably because it felt good at the level of ego,*

not to mention the money. But all of that created false expectations that he couldn't live up to. So he led a secret life. And in the confines of his own solitude and isolation, his shadow emerged. When you have to live up to an image that is not you, then sooner or later that image is defiled. Then everyone becomes enraged and many people end up getting hurt.

"YESTERDAY IS HISTORY, TOMORROW IS A MYSTERY, TODAY is a gift. That's why it's called the present."

I'm not entirely sure where this corny axiom comes from, but I've seen it on greeting cards, bumper stickers, T-shirts, mouse pads, and at least one tattoo. Google it and almost nine million entries will appear, along with references to Emily Dickinson, Bob Marley, Joan Rivers, Lil Wayne, and a 1902 book called *Sun Dials and Roses of Yesterday.*

I have no idea who first said these words, but I do know that Master Oogway delivers the line with particular elegance in the animated film *Kung Fu Panda.* I know this because I've watched the movie every morning for the last six months. At 5:30 a.m.

I've been assigned "morning duty" in our house, a shift that entails waking up with the boy, letting the dog out in the backyard, changing the boy's diaper, letting the dog back into the house, giving her a treat, pouring milk and cereal for the boy, making waffles, and then all three of us (boy, dad, dog) plunking down in front of *Kung Fu Panda.* At 5:30 a.m.

Despite my efforts to mix it up—introduce a little *Horton Hears a Who* or *Madagascar 2* or maybe SportsCenter—Krishu's loyalty to *Panda* is steadfast. We cannot deviate from the routine. It's amazing, really. Krishu can watch *Panda* every single morning as if it's the first time. He laughs at all of Po's jokes, recoils when Tai Lung escapes from prison, and edges forward on the couch when Tigress, Mantis, Monkey, and Viper ready themselves to accept Tai Lung's combative challenge. Krishu knows what's coming—even anticipates it—nevertheless, he plays each moment over and over with an enthusiasm that is nothing short of amazing.

The same can't be said for me. Maybe that's why I've dreamed up an alternative, more *Dark Knight*-ish story line, one in which Tai Lung *actually* succeeds in his coup to unseat Master Shifu. In this version, Tai Lung takes over the world, disrupting the spiritual equilibrium of the planet and propelling it into an apocalyptic darkness, like being forced to sit in the oversized chairs at Starbucks while staring at drab pagan artwork for all eternity.

In this Armageddon, spiritual disciplines and martial arts like kung fu, karate, and judo would have to be mined, reawakened, and reimagined, and the warriors who mastered them would be the planet's last hope to possibly reignite civilization from the barista-driven madness it had become. It's just a thought.

The trade-off for my doing morning duty is that by 6:30 I can return Krishu to bed to snuggle with his mama while I mount my flashy new road bike and head out into the canyons for a semi-strenuous bike ride. The point of this obsessive riding (aside from getting out of the house) is to train for an intensive bike trip I had planned in Italy. My brother-in-law, senior to me by about five years, had recruited me into this boys' club comprised mostly of guys like him: successful professional investors, bankers, and real estate magnates whose jobs had suddenly become a lot less busy on account of a receding economy. When we weren't actually out on our bikes, forming amateur race formations, comparing slick new pedals, gears, and other components I was only just becoming familiar with, we were sharing YouTube videos and links to maps and commentaries that showed just how impossible our upcoming Italian endeavor really was.

Aside from the rigorous physical training and mental games spurred by YouTube, I had also adjusted my diet considerably. Carbs and sugars were strictly monitored. Proteins were consumed in plenty and calories—once so forbidden—were now most welcome to provide energy for the training rides that included steep climbs up the canyons of Santa Monica and Malibu. Our kitchen had turned into a veritable laboratory, the cabinets packed with colorful powders and thick protein bars. I spent early mornings mixing, shaking, blending them like a sorcerer and concocting elaborate molasses-like shakes that I'd muscle down as Candice, Krishu, and even Cleo watched aghast. It was worth it, I told myself. After all, didn't the packaging promise that these supplements would energize my body and help it recover after particularly grueling training sessions?

The more I thought about all of this training and the collateral effect, the less clear I was about why exactly I was doing it. I knew that while I enjoyed biking, it didn't come close to stirring the competitive juices I once felt when I played pickup basketball games at the local playground, recreation I had given up only months ago after chronic knee problems forced me off the court. Biking was one of the few sports I could come up with that didn't involve high impact on my creaky joints. Still, there was nothing really competitive about the sport, just long, arduous rides, sometimes with steady climbs up hills that required their own strategy to conquer.

If anything, scaling these hills required quieting the mind and pacing thoughts over long, taxing periods. That sort of mental training was new for me, akin to meditation, which I was familiar with, but very different from the sort of instinctive movements that came with basketball. Taking on steep hills too aggressively risked overexertion, sabotaging reserve energy that was required for longer rides. This recalibration of my athletic life—always a big part of my existence—was significant for me and something I was still adjusting to even as the Italy trip crept closer. So even as I fixated on how I was going to do it, I still hadn't fully resolved *why.*

My father noted my sudden obsession with riding.

"You're really into it, huh?" he remarked one morning as he brewed his coffee.

"I guess so." I shrugged, still ambivalent.

"I know why," he said as he poured hazelnut creamer into his cup. "You're getting old."

I looked at him dubiously.

"You used to just put on your sneakers, pick up a ball, and go play." He stirred the creamer into his coffee. "From when you were about eleven years old to just a few months ago. Now you have an expensive bike with expensive bike clothes packed with strange gels and liquids, preparing for an expensive trip halfway across the planet just to exercise." He shrugged and sipped his coffee.

"Um, I don't think—"

"You're too young to have a midlife crisis," he determined. "But the writing is on the wall. You're going to Italy to exercise."

I stared at him blankly, unsure of what to say. My first thought was to just be impressed that he actually had any memories of me when I was eleven years old. Not the generic age of ten, nor the broad swath of being a teenager, but eleven. That was pretty good.

I shook my head as I filled my water bottle. "I don't know if that's it," I mumbled.

"That's it." He nodded, convinced. "While our existence in the cosmic context is barely a parenthesis in eternity, at times it can seem interminable for those of us enduring it. So we seek ways to distract ourselves." He changed the subject. "It's a nice bike. How much did it cost?"

No way I was going there. "I forget."

"Sure." He nodded again as he shuffled out of the kitchen. "Have a good ride."

ON THE EXPENSIVE business class flight to Italy, I thought more about my conversation with Papa. Maybe he was right. Deep inside, I knew there was a part of me that was feeling an itch. Back at home, I had become a creature of habit adhering to a routine. My daily schedule had become rigid and predictable. Where not long ago, I used to gallivant around the world, hanging out with and interviewing narco-traffickers and terrorists (or freedom fighters, depending on your POV), now I was a guy with a wife, a kid, a dog, a mortgage, obligations and commitments, and a new expensive indulgence. As much as I adored my family and valued my life, I saw it leading down an even more predictable path—more kids, more dogs, higher mortgage payments, school fees, increased obligations and commitments. What was I going to do to counteract all of this? Get a more expensive bike? Go to Saint-Jean-de-Maurienne next year to retrace the Tour de France? Was that what my life was becoming? Who *I* was becoming?

"Mr. Chopra, can I offer you a cocktail?" the flight attendant interrupted my rapidly evolving crisis. She had been chatty when I first boarded the flight and had helped me identify all the perks of my fancy leather seat. Already I had put to good use the chichi moisturizer and lip balm, donned the soft socks, and planned on using the silky blindfold. She feigned great interest when I informed her of the purpose of my trip. My gaze lingered on her attractive smile and raven-colored hair for a beat. This is where the midlife crisis inevitably goes, isn't it?

I shook myself out of it. "No, thanks."

I recalibrated my mind. I needed to stop thinking about the distant future, filled with anxiety-inducing images of suburban blight. I had more immediate problems, namely an exhaustive physical conquest I still wasn't convinced I was ready for. And it wasn't only the physical challenge. A large part of the energy committed to the imminent ride was the hype surrounding it. Not just in terms of the six months or so of intensive physical training leading up to it, but in the discussion and research around it. I'd already collected a veritable archive of video footage on my computer, meant both to inspire and intimidate. In the immediate days before I left for the trip, when I dropped by the local bike store to load up on additional paraphernalia, I mentioned my trip to the store manager.

"Really?" he said, more than a little perplexed.

"Yeah, really." I nodded back.

He laughed and shook his head. What was that supposed to mean?

I pressed him but he wouldn't let on. "No point in getting stressed about it now."

Too late for that. Some of the mountainous passes on our agenda were amongst the toughest rides in the world. They came with fancy Italian names like the Stelvio, Gavia, and Motirolo, and were spoken about in awe by those who knew. While most of the rides themselves would likely last only four to five hours at most, the discussion around them could evidently last months. Each was cloaked in legend and lore. Each aroused anxiety and intimidation in amateur riders and veterans alike. Like the guy who ran the bike shop. I was suitably stressed.

Upon landing in Milan and embarking on the three-and-a-half-hour car ride north into the Dolomite region, I saw the hills we'd be scaling. They were impressive to say the least, terrifying to say it plainly. From afar, they appeared majestic, their peaks shrouded in clouds. As afternoon turned to night and it became more difficult to actually see how far out the road in front of us climbed, I found myself staring out the side of the window, inspecting the angle of the road as it rushed by and counting "Mississippis" in my head, trying to get a gauge on just how lengthy these slopes were, how long it would take to ride them. The higher the counts rose, the more nervous I became.

Figuring the best thing I could do to suppress my nerves was to distract myself, I turned my attention to Ian, the sinewy instructor we had hired to be our guide for the week. But he did little to quell my fears. After some obligatory chitchat about movies and other forgettable fare, the conversation turned to riding, little more than a passing fad to me, but a full-on passion for him. When I described some of what I had heard about the epic rides we were to encounter and the nerves that accompanied them, he responded solemnly. "Don't think about any of that," he intoned. "Seriously, it can really paralyze you to think that way. Just stay focused on the road in front of you."

Okay, I nodded. My first impression of Ian was that he was a pretty relaxed guy. This turn into serious land felt somewhat abrupt. While his point was to *not* think about the rides coming up just hours away, his sudden earnest tone did the exact opposite. "I'm screwed" reverberated in my head the way my father once taught me to silently repeat my mantra, or secret sound, when I meditated.

A few hours later we at last arrived at the charming hotel that would serve as our home base for the next few days. I called Candice to check in.

"Are you nervous about the ride tomorrow?" she asked.

"Apparently we shouldn't be talking about it," I told her.

"Seriously?" I could picture her brow furrowed. "Why?"

"Makes the ride impossible or something. I don't know." I shook my head. "Biker talk."

"That makes sense," Candice agreed.

"Really?" I was the one grimacing now. "Since when did you become Lance Armstrong?"

She laughed. "I don't know. Focus on the race, not the finish line. The journey is the destination. That's probably something your dad would say."

"Or Nike," I shot back. "How's the boy?"

"Good," she replied. "Entertaining his grandmother."

Candice's mother had traveled from her home in Atlanta to lend Candice a helping hand. Preparing his meals, changing his diapers, reading him books, giving him a bath, watching *Kung Fu Panda*; there were a lot of routines for which Candice needed coverage. Her mom was more than capable of mastering them all. But more than anything, *Wai pó* (the Chinese term by which Krishu referred to his maternal grandmother) was his long-lost play pal. She indulged him far more than anyone else, thereby becoming his favorite person. He ordered her around, demanding foods on off hours—cereal at night, sandwiches in the morning—as if to test her boundaries and find his own.

Bad timing. Prompted by a great deal of pressure from Candice's newly formed mommy mafia, she and I had in recent weeks begun the great potty training challenge. All of the parenting books had been consulted and all of them agreed, the more we could add structure around Krishu's life, create a reliable routine for him and a set of expectations for him to rely on, the smoother the process would go. So started Krishu's cultural indoctrination, as my father later described it, into the ways of our world.

"It starts with regulating your biology. It ends with regulating everything else until you're just a bundle of conditioned reflexes."

Like many of Papa's statements, this sounded like something the Unabomber would say. Oh well.

Early on, Krishu seemed to take to the new routine, happy to park it on his little plastic potty chair as long as one of us was willing to park it alongside him and read him a story. He even managed to deliver the goods once or twice in the first week, earning accolades from family members with whom we shared the joyous news.

"He's really advanced for his age," my mother commended.

"A total prodigy," Candice's father agreed.

Those initial deposits into the potty chair set us on a dangerous path of false expectations. Candice and I were convinced that the books had it wrong, that this was not a process that would take months and was inevitably fraught with setbacks. It would take just days for our metabolic boy-genius to master the tao of poo, as Master Oogway might call it. Alas, it was as if Krishu sensed this sudden pressure for him to mature too quickly, and soon enough his defiance kicked in. He had no real interest in our desire to assimilate him in a world where potties were deposited in some strange porcelain throne and flushed away. He was perfectly happy with the current system where he'd do his business whenever and wherever he needed to and we'd clean up after him. It had worked out fine for him so far.

"How's the potty training coming?" I asked Candice warily.

"Not so great," she replied. She blamed it on *Wai pó's* arrival and her indulgences of the boy. We both knew the real reasons ran much deeper, that our son was the Mangal Pandey, India's legendary mutineer, of potty training. If given a chance, he would lead a revolt of as many two-year-olds as he could find to resist this horrible custom called potty training. He had played a leading hand in similar rebellions in the sandbox. Still, it was far easier to pin the blame on Grandma.

"Eh." I shrugged, half a world away, resigned to letting the kid figure it out. It was consistent with my larger parenting philosophy. Eventually, either because it just felt uncomfortable or because of the inevitable cultural awkwardness of being a teenager who shat in his pants, Krishu would beg us to be potty trained. I felt the same way about his eating and sleeping. When he got hungry enough, he'd eat. When he got tired enough, he'd sleep. Why such pressure to create elaborate rituals and routines to trick him into stuff he instinctively defied? Alas, more theories that never stood a chance with my wife.

"Does he miss me?" I asked.

"Do you want me to lie to you or tell you the truth?"

"Go ahead and lie."

"He's really missing you and asking for you constantly." Impressive.

I knew in fact that with *Wai pó* in the house, he'd hardly have noticed I was gone. "What about Cleo?"

This time Candice didn't even bother to lay out the options. "She's really missing you and asking for you constantly!"

"She'd better . . . Ungrateful bitch."

Candice laughed and then added affectionately, "You are, aren't you?" Clearly Cleo had rolled over by Candice's side and was reaping loving rubs.

"I wouldn't lose any sleep over it," Candice reminded me. "You know Cleo. As soon as you're back, she'll love you more than ever. Her mind works on what's right in front of her."

"Yeah," I lamented. "But why can't she be like those dogs you always hear about? You know, that sit in front of the door waiting for their master? That get all depressed and moody because the thing they care most about in the world is that one person who's not there?"

"Ha! Cleo? Think again."

"I guess." I shrugged. It's actually one of Cleo's greatest attributes—her ability to focus her attention on the present moment without being distracted by anything else.

"I miss you," Candice said, her voice once again suspiciously seductive.

"Liar!"

"Watch it, Lance!" she warned. "You'd better get some sleep for that big ride tomorrow that we can't talk about and you shouldn't think about."

"Okay," I said. *"Ciao."*

"Ooh," she purred. "Very Italian."

AS I SETTLED into my cozy hotel room in Bormio, Italy, my cell phone rang. I picked it up to find my father on the other end of the line.

"How was the flight?" he asked.

"Expensive," I replied. He laughed.

"I talked to Mom." He paused. "Nana's doing much better. His condition is stable. He'll probably go home in a few days."

Stable is such a strange term if you really think about it. Surely it's better than "critical" or "life-threatening," but far short of where you want to be, if you ask me.

"Okay," I said hesitantly. "What does that mean?"

"It means let's take one day at a time." Papa reverted into doctor verbiage. "He should be fine. But I don't want to say much."

Who knew Papa was such a voodoo doctor, as if what he said would somehow disrupt the delicate balance of Nana's recovery.

"Is Mom okay?" I asked, changing tack. If for some reason she wasn't, it would be a telling sign. My mom is notoriously even-keeled.

"She's okay. A bit emotional, you know? It's her father after all."

A curveball. On the one hand, the fact that my mother was "emotional" was concerning. The inclusion, however, of the "it's her father after all" bit was a variable. I was unsure how to reconcile this.

"Don't get worked up about it." Papa interrupted my thoughts. "No one can control the future. You'll wear yourself out trying. Just have the intention that Nana will be fine and let go."

There it was again, the whole intention, attention, detachment equation. Sounded simple enough, yet enormously difficult in execution.

"I'll try," I said unconvincingly.

"Trying won't work," Papa reprimanded.

Right, *a fish doesn't try to swim, it just does. A bird doesn't try to fly, it just does. You don't try to walk, you just do.* Between Papa and Yoda, these were axioms I had grown up with. But it didn't make things any easier.

"How's baby?" This had become my father's new bailout move whenever he was unsure where to steer a conversation.

"Good," I said. "Potty training is not going so hot."

This too stumped him. I'd be willing to bet my every last penny that my father had no involvement in my potty training when I was a toddler.

"Yeah, it's never easy." Wow—good recovery. "What about Cleo?" he asked.

I laughed, impressed. The fact that he remembered her name, let alone was concerned about how she was doing, signified a genuine and growing connection between the two of them.

"She's great," I answered. "Now that Candice's mom is there, she'll actually get to go on some long walks every day."

"How often does she see Candice's mom?" Papa inquired.

I thought about it. Candice's mom visited us about every six months or so. I informed Papa.

"Do you think," Papa started, "that if you opened up Cleo's skull and looked at her brain, you would find that memory of Candice's mom?"

I hoped it was a rhetorical question. "Don't get any ideas."

"The brain, for both humans and dogs," he noted, "does not store memories. There's no archive system for them inside your brains. Memories exist as possibilities nonlocally in a central plain of existence."

"Let me give this a shot," I offered. "It's the difference between storing data on your hard drive versus storing it on the server."

Pause.

"The real difference between Cleo and us is her ability to access the server with minimal disruption."

This time I demanded a translation.

"It's pretty simple. Animals react and do not reflect on their reactions. They draw on their own memories and the memories of their species, but they are not tainted by nor twisted around emotions."

It made me think. Even if a few months or a year had passed, as soon as Candice's mom walked through the door, Cleo was all over her, leaping up onto her, excitedly seeking affection.

"So you don't think Cleo is motivated by memories?" I inquired. "I mean, she clearly reacts instinctively to a lot of things."

"There's a big difference," Papa responded quickly. "To be reactive to your past, to memories, is to be a prisoner of them. That's what most people do—play victim to their past experiences. Being instinctive is totally different.

"Instincts are based on our collective memory or karma. The alchemy of all of our past experiences manifests in the instincts of our species. Instincts rely on that reservoir of past experiences.

"Even humans—no one has to teach us how to fall in love for the first time. Not because we have any memory of it or how great the experience is, but because at the right moment, it *feels* right.

"The problem is that we create barriers in our own lives, condition ourselves. That first moment of falling in love creates a memory that we then will go back to for the rest of our lives. It creates an expectation of what love should be like in the future. That's when things get complicated.

"Cleo's beyond the complications," Papa concluded.

It was a lot to digest. "Do you really think humans are capable of that?" I asked.

This time Papa didn't respond with the hesitation as he had before. In fact, he didn't respond at all.

"Papa?" I prodded. "Are you there?"

Another beat passed before he finally spoke. "Turn on your TV," Papa said, his tone decidedly altered.

"Why?" I scrambled to locate the remote. "What?"

Another pause. "They're saying that Michael Jackson may be dead."

. . .

I FIRST MET Michael when I was fifteen. My father had been introduced to him by Elizabeth Taylor, who was a frequent visitor to an alternative health center in western Massachusetts where my father had become the medical director. The more Ms. Taylor learned about my father and the spiritual material that he was engaged in, the more she became convinced that Michael would be fascinated by him. While she was most interested in the spa-like resources that the health center offered, not to mention the fact that it was so removed from Hollywood and the chaos that came with it, my father recalled that she thought Michael would be more attracted to "all that other magical stuff" that my father spoke about— like meditation, consciousness, and karma.

She was right. Michael became family from the moment he and Papa met. And it wasn't just the "magic stuff" that he was attracted to; it was the "normal stuff" as well. Just a few months after my father and Michael met, Michael invited him to his Neverland ranch just near Santa Barbara.

Papa mentioned his upcoming trip one night over dinner. He was so casual he might have been discussing the weather.

"How long a drive is it from Los Angeles to Santa Barbara? I have a meeting in LA next week and then might make a trip to Michael Jackson's ranch. He wants to see me."

Mallika and I stared at him in disbelief.

"What?" he asked as we struggled to find words.

"Michael . . . ?" I uttered.

"Jackson . . . ?" she completed.

Papa nodded. "Do you want to come with me?"

Mallika was heartbroken. She desperately wanted to go, but was scheduled to leave the following morning on some do-gooder mission to the Dominican Republic. Something about spending the summer digging latrines. I, on the other hand, had no such philanthropic agenda. My plans centered around a summer's worth of bleacher bumming at Fenway Park.

I played it cool, though. After all, I was fifteen, the pinnacle of teen arrogance and attitude. I wore Cross Colors and Adidas. I played varsity basketball and totally *felt* J. D. Salinger. I couldn't react the way I wanted to: "Are you f'ing kidding me? Hell yes, I'll go with you to meet Michael f'ing Jackson."

Instead, I shrugged. "Yeah, that sounds cool. I'll come with . . ."

Like many in my generation, I had grown up as a devotee of Michael Jackson. It wasn't just his music that I obsessed over, it was *him*. It was the *Thriller* video that inspired a consecutive string of seven Halloween costumes and the purchase of a red leather jacket that I sliced up to resemble the one MJ wore in the iconic video. It was the *Billie Jean* performance at the Motown twenty-fifth Anniversary special that inspired the purchase of half a dozen penny loafers. It was the glove he wore that prompted me to buy a skier's insulation glove—the closest thing I could find to resemble the one he wore. And there was the black fedora that I made my parents buy me and that I wore constantly until it resembled something more suited to Indiana Jones than Michael Jackson. I looked like a real idiot wearing that oversized hat at the age of eleven and yet, because almost everyone else also idolized Michael Jackson, it was cool.

Michael Jackson *was* cool. The way he mastered the stage or rocked out a stadium with such superhero-like power and sheer talent, but then seemed so vulnerable and human off it . . . cool.

Having grown up with the guru to the stars, I've been lucky to meet a lot of famous people. And if there's one thing I've learned it's that they're usually not as intimidating in person as their celebrity may have made them out to be. Over time, I guess I realized that it was less about them and more about *us* and our expectations. We idolize celebrities, create icons out of them, and are disappointed, even angered, when they don't live up to the standards we've created.

I'd experienced this up close and personal. There was the bestselling author I'd idolized in high school, whom I met at a dinner party and who became rankled when talking about Barnes & Noble and how they didn't place his books at eye level on their shelves. As if that wasn't enough, all through dinner he just bitched and moaned about Amazon's shipping policies to the point that it was really tragic. Knowing how much he despised the good people who brought his books to the public—and worse, seeing just how petty he was—made it hard to appreciate the words he put on a page after that. There was the sexy actress whom I fantasized about until I overheard her refer to the health center staff as "hired help not worth minimum wage." After that I could never, well, fantasize about her in the same way.

In the "self-help" world, which over the years we had become even more embedded in, the ironies were even more intense. Relationship experts whose embattled marriages were full of scandal and infidelity. Nutrition gurus who hid out in the back of restaurants carb loading, chasing them down with soft drinks. Advocates of "simplifying one's life" who traveled with entourages that made pro athletes look like amateurs.

Not so with Michael.

He was everything I had ever imagined and so much more. We became friends over the years. Family. I would learn that not only was he an incredibly dynamic and brilliant artist, a celebration of divine-like talent, but also a deeply conflicted and agonized soul. Michael may have been a man whose head was often in the clouds, so disconnected from the reality that "ordinary people" experienced, but he was also someone who felt human emotions in the deepest way I'd ever witnessed.

Years after I met him, I matriculated at the prestigious Ivy League school Columbia University—largely because of a college recommendation he wrote. Michael lived mostly in New York City, high atop the Four Seasons Hotel in the penthouse, and I'd visit him regularly, just hanging out, sometimes collaborating on some projects he was working on, constantly trying to draw him out from the isolating cocoon that he and his advisers had wrapped around him. Usually I'd fail. To compensate me for some of the contributions I'd made to his projects, he'd pay me in cash, pulling a literal sack of bills from behind the toilet where he kept it hidden, and slipping me a couple grand. I'd proceed to call my college friends, who'd hop on the subway and meet me downtown so we could spend that same cash on what mattered most to us at the time: strippers.

More time passed. Michael went from iconic rock star, the greatest talent the world may have ever seen, to scandal-plagued celebrity. His face was literally falling apart—the result of not only self-inflicted surgeries to combat some of his deeper psychological issues, but a skin disease that few knew about. The press alleged that he was a race-hater or a freak, charges that made Michael alternatively melancholy and furious. And of course there were the even more devastating allegations of sexual impropriety with young boys that would for a time taint all of his past glories. For me, where I once proudly showed off that I had met MJ when I was fifteen years old, it was now a sheepish throwaway line that I muttered under my breath for fear of the raised eyebrows and smirks it would trigger.

After the storm clouds of the scandals passed, Michael entered a new stage of his life, and I soon followed: fatherhood. We took decidedly different roads to the same destination. Whereas I did it the old-fashioned way, Michael literally manufactured a family, one that would love him in a way that no one else ever had. It was easy to see from the way he was with his three kids that they were the one thing in his life he valued above all else. Years after he had already started his family, Candice gave birth to Krishu. Michael called me and said, "See—I told you so, Igger" (his nickname for me. He had nicknames for everyone. "*Starbucks*," you know who you are), "it's the greatest thing you'll ever know."

I actually asked him to be Krishu's godfather, but ominously he said he didn't think he'd be a good one. "I think you should find someone who'd be better at it," he confessed. "There are too many bad things in my life he shouldn't learn."

He did nickname Krishu "the Chindian," though, and checked in once every few weeks to make sure that Candice and I were speaking multiple languages around him.

"Michael," I'd tell him early on, "he's just a few months old."

"Doesn't matter," he'd respond, "he's smarter than all of us. Make sure you keep it that way."

All the while in the last few years of his life, even as he was gaining greater emotional and spiritual fulfillment than he ever had through his life with his children, Michael was struggling. Those close to him knew it, and yet, despite repeated attempts, there wasn't much anyone could really do. Once again, he had become exceedingly skillful at building that cocoon of isolation around him, especially because he thought he had a secret he didn't want anyone to know.

Just a few weeks before I had left for Italy, he had called me in the middle of the night, as he often did. He sounded clearheaded and on point. He'd heard about the fate of my journalist friend Laura Ling, imprisoned in North Korea, and wanted to know if I knew any details the news was not reporting. (Based on his own experiences with many journalists, he didn't trust them all that much.) When I told him there wasn't much information to be had, that North Korea was ruled over by a totalitarian regime that controlled the press, he paused. He told me he'd seen pictures of Kim Jong-il, the "Dear Leader" of North Korea who ruled the isolated nation with an iron fist. He noticed that he often wore military jackets, similar to the ones that Michael wore when he went out in public or performed.

"Do you think he's a fan of mine?" Michael proposed.

I shrugged in the darkness of my room. "I don't know."

"If so, maybe I can help in some way."

I promised him I'd look into it.

"Okay." He thanked me. "I hope they're doing all right." He had read somewhere that both Laura and her colleague Euna were likely being kept in isolation. "Being by yourself like that is not easy, isolated from people, from time."

I nodded, not knowing really what to say.

"Say hi to the Chindian," he whispered. "Good night."

AFTER I HUNG UP with my father, I paced around my Italian hotel room. I turned back to the television and flipped through the channels. Every network imaginable was covering the news that Michael Jackson was being transported to a Los Angeles hospital. Most had backed off the earlier headline that he was already dead and resigned themselves to the more nebulous description of his being in a coma and in critical condition. I knew the notorious death watch was probably under way, with satellite trucks parked outside the hospital, Michael's homes in Los Angeles and Neverland, his parents' famous Encino compound, and more, eager for news and reaction to the slightest bit of rumor.

Sitting in my hotel room, staring at the television—I had settled on an Italian news network that I couldn't even really understand—I watched with a growing pit in my stomach. A grainy and shaky video loop from the gossip website TMZ depicted frenzied paramedics rushing a slight figure on a gurney into a waiting ambulance. These images would emerge as the final ones of the great Michael Jackson. More video now caught a growing vigil of fans outside the legendary Cedars-Sinai Medical Center in Beverly Hills. The reporter rattled on in Italian, her voice almost tripping over itself while she relayed whatever the latest bit of news was. My cell phone was already buzzing with text messages and e-mails, friends eager to get an inside scoop if I had one. I glanced at the alarm clock again. It was now well after ten p.m. We were supposed to be up and out on the bikes in the early morning for our first grueling ride. Suddenly I wasn't so sure that I'd be staying much longer in Italy, let alone making the start time. Conflicting thoughts raced through my mind—whether or not I should be sticking it out or rushing home. All the while that pit in my stomach kept growing, the suspicion solidifying that no matter what the news was saying about Michael's condition, my own intuition was more reliable.

In an instant I made a single choice: to turn off the TV and my phone. The combination of jet lag, nervous anticipation for the ride, and this gut-wrenching news had unsteadied me. I sensed that tomorrow would be that much more emotionally chaotic, but separating now and then were a few short hours where I could isolate myself and not confront it all. It was less an intellectual decision than an instinctive one.

As I lay in bed a few minutes later, I thought about Michael, the first time we met, the summer I traveled with him as he toured Europe, and of the times we'd spent together since then. I felt a heaviness in my heart and tried to find more of the mostly humorous encounters that Michael and I shared through the years—the time we snuck out of his Los Angeles apartment on Halloween and visited a nightclub where he danced so feverishly that the whole crowd stopped and started cheering him—this anonymous man in a Godzilla mask. Or the time in a New York City recording studio when he told the rapper Ice-T that I was his bodyguard. Ice-T sized me up and told Michael he could help him "upgrade" if he wanted to get serious about his protection.

But I couldn't steer my own emotions away from the sadness I felt growing inside. "Let go of the illusion of control," Master Shifu reminded me. So I employed a different tact. I decided to just go ahead and feel sad. To not try and dodge the emotions, but rather "take ownership" of them, as Dr. Phil might suggest, and let them wash through me. Within five minutes, I was immersed in a deep, hard slumber.

THE FOLLOWING MORNING I woke with a start. I didn't need an alarm clock or anything else to wrestle me from my surprisingly restful sleep. I stared at the television screen, determining whether or not I should switch it on. Instead I turned to my cell phone and powered it up. Being overseas, I had the option of whether I wanted to turn on my "mail settings" and download e-mail.

Before I could decide, the phone rang. It was Papa.

"How are you?" he asked.

"You know . . ." I stopped, unsure what to say.

"They confirmed the death not too long ago," he said softly.

"Right." I nodded. Inside I felt a profound sadness, though an equally profound lack of shock.

"I think you should stay in Italy and do your bike ride," Papa suggested without my even prompting it.

"Really?" It had crossed my mind again that maybe I should call it off and head home.

"It's going to be a circus here," Papa countered. "I've already gotten calls from every news outlet you can imagine. Already did Larry King. They're asking for you."

"Yeah," I murmured, not surprised. The thought of rushing back to the growing media frenzy was not appealing.

"I don't know the first thing about biking," Papa interceded again. "But if I were you, I would get on the bike and just focus on the road in front of you."

Not surprisingly, Deepak did know biking. As it turns out, his advice was the same sage wisdom offered by the experts. Never try to conquer the race, just take one stage at a time. Don't even worry about the whole stage, break it down into sections and ride it modularly. Listen to the greatest riders and they'll tell you, they don't even think in sections as much as they just look downward where the wheel spins on the road. Sometimes they'll find the traffic lines in the road and use them to help find their rhythm and pace, until everything else—the course, the other riders, even the time itself—falls away. It's the same experience the greatest athletes use to describe being "in the zone" or "the runner's high" when all the details fade away and they become one with everything around them, including themselves. It's in fact the state of awareness that the great scriptures, both East and West, describe.

"I am the alpha and the omega, the beginning and the end, the first and the last," the Bible depicts.

"I am their beginning, their being, their end," Lord Krishna chronicles himself in the *Bhagavad Gita*.

Master Oogway concurs: "You are too concerned with what was and what will be."

I thought for a moment about the road ahead, of my father and my friend. I thought about my mother and Nana, of Candice and Krishu, and of how life is so fleeting, how it's gone in the blink of an eye, the veritable parenthesis in eternity.

We go from potty training to *being regular*. We wrap ourselves up in a web of expectation, anticipation, and memory and we find comfort in it because it offers a sense of stability and predictability. We chart out our lives with goals and codes. We plan. We prepare. And even those of us who do get those rare and powerful moments of being fully rooted *in the present* find that it can be fraught with perils. For when they are out of it—like my friend Michael Jackson—they find that ordinary existence lacks the same high.

Papa broke the silence. "Remember when Michael took us to his studio on that first visit to Neverland?" Papa recollected. "And he put on 'Billie Jean' and started dancing?"

Michael was almost bashful at first, just nodding his head to the beat of the music. But within minutes, as if he couldn't control himself, he was snapping and moving to the hard beat of the bass, dancing fluidly like only he could.

"It was beautiful," Papa described. "Because he was *in the moment*. He wasn't just the dancer—he was the dance and the music itself."

I did remember.

five

Do you know who Miley Cyrus is?
No. Who is she?
Do you know who Hannah Montana is?
Isn't she Tara's friend?
Yeah, sort of.

MY EIGHT-YEAR-OLD NIECE, TARA, IS A SPECIAL KID. THE oldest among a trio that includes her younger sister, Leela, and my son, Krishu, she takes her elder role seriously. She'll often recall the rigors of years two through five when watching her younger siblings.

"Let him be scared," she once advised me when the kids and I sat huddled together on the couch watching *Finding Nemo*. Krishu had bristled when the shark showed up and was chasing down Nemo's dad, Marlin, and loyal friend Dory. "It's okay to be afraid once in a while because then you know how people sometimes feel in the real world when bad things happen."

The mentor role suits Tara. She is thoughtful and contemplative. And because she feels things deeply and seems acutely aware of what's going on, the adults in the family are particularly aware of what they say when she's around.

It's common lore in our family that Tara only really started speaking when she was almost three, quite late by common standards and far later than her siblings reached the same milestone. Most explain this by noting that first children don't have the same level of interaction with elder kids that their younger siblings do. Tara explains it differently: "I was a thoughtful child."

Inquisitive too, as the question mark has always been her favorite form of punctuation. These days Tara is adept at picking up on tone, so we have to be mindful not just of what we say, but of how we say it.

"Why did Candy Mami (what she calls Candice) look at you that way when you told her not to eat that cheesecake?

"Did you mean it when you said you weren't ever going to talk to my mom again?

"Why did you tell your friend that that lady at Coffee Bean looked like a *bad* girl?"

Did I mention that she's eight years old?

More than just Mallika and Sumant's baby girl, Tara was the family's baby, a firstborn treasure that all of us would cherish in a special way. That included Cleo, who got her literal first licks in on Tara within days of her entering the world. It was January of 2002 and the imminent arrival of Mallika's baby kept us all close at hand. Mallika's delivery was a difficult one that ultimately ended up in her having to undergo an emergency C-section while my teary-eyed mother, anxiety-ridden father, and I waited for the good word to be delivered by my pale-faced brother-in-law. When the all clear at last came from him that Tara was healthy and Mallika would recover fine with some added days of rest, we rejoiced.

When Tara arrived home from the hospital a few days later, I was unsure whether or not I should bring Cleo over to the house to meet her. At ten pounds, and with no real history of aggression or violence, there wasn't any reason not to, and yet I found myself hesitant to take the risk. Candice, likewise, expressed her concern. Both of us loved Cleo to no end, but that didn't necessarily mean we trusted her entirely. What was the rush anyway? we reasoned. Tara was going to be around for a very long time and eventually she and Cleo would meet when things settled down—whatever that meant in the context of a newborn's life.

"On the contrary," my father demanded, surprising us all at the time, "bring the dog immediately. Let's not make any assumptions and prejudge their relationship."

On the contrary. In anticipation of Tara's arrival, Papa had been preparing for her the only way he knew—by reading intensive amounts of research on how best to nurture a child's consciousness from the very earliest stages of existence. He had big plans for Tara—using the word *perfection* not so sparingly when discussing what he envisioned for her.

"Just look at her," he said to me less than a day after she was born. "She's absolutely perfect. She's a real star—just like her name."

I smiled, reminding him that most grandparents perceived their grandchildren—especially the first ones—as being *perfect*.

"No." He shook his head vehemently as if I were missing a most obvious point. "She's not like other babies." He surveyed dismissively the rest of the babies in the unit, and came back to Tara with a smile warming his face. "Tara will change the world."

As part of this expansive ambition and strategy, Papa had come upon research indicating that infants' exposure to animals at an early stage—notably dogs—had hugely beneficial effects.

"There's a lot of data that suggests that infants who grow up around pets make for better leaders. Their sense of compassion and empathy for other beings is cemented at an emotional level. Bring the dog immediately," he ordered again, as if fearing we were already getting a late start on her leadership training.

I remained wary.

Papa turned to science. "Studies now show that kids who grow up with dogs in the house have a reduced likelihood of developing certain allergies and even asthma. The fact that dogs are dirty animals and track dirt and allergens into the house is a good thing," he assured us all. "They stimulate and strengthen the baby's immune system."

This was consistent with his theory that babies were way over-immunized in the West. On the great parent debate of inoculations, he therefore fell somewhere in the middle—get the basics but then throw caution to the wind and let the baby and the world—or in this case Cleo—find their own equilibrium.

"Don't let the dog have a bath," he reminded me.

"Okay," I said, though I had Cleo washed anyway.

I remember clearly that first time Cleo and Tara met. Mallika was hopped up on painkillers and Sumant was at work, so parent paranoia was not a factor. Tara—just days old—was propped up in a little chair bouncing lightly and rocking back and forth. Like most babies at that stage, she was up and cooing, or as my father liked to describe her, "Like Buddha awake and aware of her own implicit enlightenment." I brought Cleo close and, as my parents carefully watched, held tightly to her leash to let her sniff out Tara from a safe distance. I wasn't taking any chances. I would let Cleo scope out the baby, but stay far enough away so that she couldn't actually make any contact. Gradually, as the pup became more comfortable with her surroundings, I released her leash some so she could poke her snout near Tara's feet.

As Cleo got her first licks in, Tara cooed and gurgled loudly. And then, shocking all of us, she reached out and stroked Cleo's snout with her tiny little hand. It was so gentle and graceful and un-baby-like, we all just stared with amazement. Even Cleo—the most frenetic of dogs—seemed calmed. She nuzzled closer to the baby, letting Tara brush her hand more over her snout, across the bridge of her nose, up her crown until her hand lay on top of Cleo's head. Cleo seemed almost entranced. In all her years, I had never seen her react like that to anyone she didn't know very well, let alone a child.

"See." My father nodded. "I told you. Tara is enlightened."

From that day forth, Tara and Cleo's relationship seemed special. As she grew from an infant to a toddler to a kid, not a day would go by that she didn't make time for Cleo. Amongst her first words were "I love Cleo." She insisted on accompanying me to the pet store once a week to buy special treats and toys. Some nights my sister would call me late, insisting that I bring Cleo over because Tara could only sleep if she was able to lay her hand on little Cleo's chest as they nuzzled together.

More recently as Tara's pre-preteen schedule got cluttered up with school, friends, and activities, she made sure Cleo wasn't left behind. Often she'd drop by the house before she went to school or alternatively in the afternoon after she was done for the day. On the weekends, we'd regularly drop Cleo off for an afternoon or even overnight at Mallika's house so she and Tara could spend a few hours together. For her part, Cleo would just follow Tara around the house wherever she went. Tara, meanwhile, would make sure to clear a spot for Cleo beside her no matter where she ultimately ended up. If she was doing homework, she'd make sure that as she dutifully practiced her handwriting with her right hand, her left was free and equally at work rubbing Cleo with affection. If she was plopping down to watch *High School Musical* or a new Bollywood movie her father had retrieved from the local Indian grocery, Cleo got an even better perk, usually earning a spot in Tara's lap. Even when it came to family time—when we all got together for dinner or were just hanging out—Cleo chose her spot and stuck close to Tara's side.

The more I witnessed Cleo and Tara's interactions, the more it brought a smile to my face because it was a reboot exactly of Mallika's relationship with Nicholas when she and I were kids. While over the years that we had him, Nicholas had become a sort of rough-and-tumble buddy of mine, always wrestling and playing, he and Mallika had developed a more affectionate and loving bond. Whereas he loved to roll around in the fallen foliage with me when summer turned to autumn or chase me as I slid down the hills after a winter snowfall, with Mallika, Nicholas always found a loving hand or warm embrace to snuggle in. As with my mother, it was no coincidence that after he died unexpectedly, Mallika would never seriously contemplate getting a dog again. The potential for hurt was too much. I knew it was difficult for her to watch Tara's bond build every day with Cleo. One part of her was witnessing her own past replay itself. Would the same ending play out as well?

I certainly hoped not.

THE RIDE THROUGH the Dolomites had been everything it was cracked up to be: physically grueling, spiritually and emotionally exhilarating. There were indeed moments as we climbed frigid peaks, and the air thinned out, that my mind drifted to Michael

and pinches of sadness crept in. But the demands of the task drew me back, kept me focused and, in many ways, happily isolated from the brewing madness seemingly everywhere else. As soon as Sumant and I arrived at the airport in Milan, preparing for the flight back to LA, I sensed that even though a week had passed since Michael's death, there was no letup in the press's covering it.

When we landed in LA, things only intensified. Rumors about how Michael had died (including *if he had really died*) were being broadcast and talked about everywhere. Was it an accident, murder, or suicide? Was it related to drugs, medical issues, or even mob-related, considering some of the huge debts Michael was alleged to have amassed?

On TV, cut and pasted documentaries and commemoratives had started to pop up everywhere. It was impossible to change channels without seeing Michael doing the moonwalk or flinging his fedora across the stage. His death was nothing short of a cultural event, and even though I recognized that at an objective level—even contributed to it in the ensuing days by appearing on shows like *Larry King Live*—I couldn't separate myself from the enormous sadness I felt inside. Though I was probably the closest in my family to Michael, we all felt the same inescapable emptiness. In addition to my mom being away in India, it was just another reason for us to circle the wagons and huddle around the dinner table every night to see if we could make one another feel better.

Even Tara was acutely aware of the relentless chatter coming from every media outlet. For her, Michael was not a supernova or family friend, nor the scandal-plagued enigma he had become for so many. He was Paris's dad. The nanny who cared for Michael's children was a close friend of Mallika's, and would bring the kids over to play. Michael's daughter, Paris, in particular, was awe-inspiring to Tara. Her sweetness, respect toward elders, general grace, and softness were all qualities Tara emulated. Tara had met Michael only once, an unremarkable encounter from what I recall, if only because of her impatience to wiggle away from the adults so that she could follow Paris around the house. These days, she moped around the house, wondering to herself what would happen to Paris and her brothers. "She must be so sad that her papa is not there anymore. I bet she's crying a lot. I'm really sad for her."

We all felt Michael's loss deeply. There was a solemnity and sadness. And there was also rage. Papa, in particular, was convinced, even before the coroner's report confirmed it, that Michael's untimely death was the result of reckless physicians who both enabled and indulged his voracious appetite for prescription drugs. Combined with his own defiance of a medical establishment that in his mind was in bed with billion-dollar drug and insurance companies, Papa became a one-man wrecking crew in the media. For him, Michael's tragic death became a flashpoint around which to raise awareness of doctors gone wild, in this case, of a physician armed *literally* with a license to kill. Not to mention the drug and insurance companies that were minting blood money off the whole sordid business.

Papa in particular saw no reason to suppress any of this conversation around the dinner table. He regarded Tara specifically as supremely mature for her age. Mallika occasionally challenged his notions of Tara's precociousness. She reminded us all that Tara was influenced subtly by a lot of what we talked about in ways that we might not even know.

"She's growing up too fast," Mallika constantly lamented, but even she knew that there was no way to truly shield Tara from the darker realities that surrounded us. It wasn't just Papa, who at least was trying to resurrect a phoenix of meaning from Michael's tragic demise. The rumors and details surrounding his death were everywhere. Television, the radio, the Internet, and every single magazine were in coverage overdrive. Who was going to control Michael's estate? Who was going to gain custody of the children? Where was he going to be buried? And increasingly, was his death just an elaborate hoax?

The specter of death was palpable in the house. It wasn't just about Michael. A nagging paranoia reigned every time the phone rang—would it be my mother with news that Nana's condition had taken a turn for the worse?

All this made its impression on Tara. While Leela and Krishu managed to carry on oblivious, hidden away in their playroom, where they alternatively played and feuded with each other, Tara's disposition drifted. When sad or hurt, her tendency was to become easily distracted and aloof. Eventually this would transform into a surreptitious defiance, the target of which was most often her mother. Mallika managed this routine carefully. She'd been warned by her friends that she needed to play this process smart, for Tara was only seven years old at the time and together they were scoping out the rules and standards by which her teens would be enacted. Candice and I regularly watched this convoluted gamesmanship and found ourselves relieved we'd had a son. I for one was no good at emotional games, too often manipulated by not just Candice, but even Cleo.

Still, despite Mallika's measured response, Tara could still push her mother's buttons, driving her patience over the edge. Sumant would attempt to come to the rescue and get slaughtered in the process. For anytime he came down on his dear daughter Tara with a modicum of discipline, she turned on the tears and all bets were off.

This evening Mallika and Tara had just tussled about Tara's sudden about-face at attending summer camp, which was to start the following morning. Months ago, Tara had insisted that she was committed to going to a local summer camp that some of her friends were veterans of. Knowing that Tara wasn't a fan of a lot of the activities listed in the camp brochure—notably camping and sports—Mallika had pressed Tara if it was something she really wanted to do.

"I have to do it!" Tara had pleaded at the time.

In defense of Tara, "had to" was indeed not what Mallika may have interpreted it to be. It was neither "want to" nor "determined to." It was likely a peer-pressure-induced obligation that Tara had assumed she needed to meet in order to keep pace with her friends. Just from occasionally covering for my sister and running Tara's morning car pool, it was obvious to me that peer pressure was already a real stress in her life. Whatever the case—perhaps friends had changed or some other trend had trumped that expensive summer camp—Tara was not just uninterested in the camp, all of a sudden she had stomachaches and other ailments that made clear she had no intention of showing up the following morning.

"If you make a commitment to doing something, then you should at least try it," Mallika advised Tara as we all sat down for our meal.

"You shouldn't ever try and force me to do things, Mom," Tara told her mother with an air of attitude. It was a warning that sent shivers through those of us who sat silently at the dinner table.

"You shouldn't ever try and threaten me," Mallika replied.

The message was sent.

Tara knew she'd crossed the line. This combined with more death conversation had left its emotional mark on her. Her eyes filled with tears. Her little shoulders slumped. "No one understands me," she announced. "Only Cleo. She's the only person who really listens, the only one who knows who I am."

With that she retreated from the dining room to her bedroom,

Cleo loyally by her side. "Dada." Krishu turned to Papa, who sat just beside him. "Tara and Cleo crying." To Krishu, Tara's tears were Cleo's tears and vice versa. "Tara want treat?" he proposed.

"No, Krishu," Papa advised him. "Tara's sad, but Cleo will make her feel better."

It was true, I thought to myself. Cleo would make Tara feel better. That's after all what she did.

IT WAS AROUND the same time that Tara was born in 2002 that Papa and I drove from Los Angeles to Santa Barbara to visit Michael at his home in Neverland again. I remember the drive vividly because Cleo joined us. Papa wasn't that fond of the idea, especially since Cleo was so desperate to lie in his lap the entire ride north along the scenic Pacific Coast Highway.

"She's probably cold," I informed him. "And she likes the way you smell."

Papa stared at me, unsure how to respond. "I'm serious." I shrugged. "The stronger you smell, the closer she likes to be to you."

"What are you saying?" Papa suddenly took on a self-conscious look.

"Papa—seriously. You know . . ." I let the words linger, unsure myself now where to take things.

Anyone who knew Papa did in fact know what I was talking about. His special mix of Body Shop musk oil, Old Spice aftershave, Crabtree & Evelyn cologne, heavy Right Guard aerosol, and Johnson & Johnson baby powder made for a formidable and aromatic cocktail.

"Why do you think I have the window open?"

Papa shook his head and readjusted carefully in his seat so as not to let Cleo fall. Even though by then Cleo had solidified her place in the family, Papa was still unsure how to act around her. The fact that he tolerated her was more or less the best thing you could say about his behavior toward her. What I was witnessing at that moment was likely the most affectionate they'd ever been.

"Do you even know if Michael likes dogs? Whether he's afraid of them? I'm not sure you should have brought the dog," Papa said.

"I don't know." I shrugged. "I mean, come on—you can't be afraid of Cleo. Look at her."

As if on cue, Cleo exhaled heavily, flopping her head over Papa's leg, her eyes still tightly shut.

"By the way, you know she has a name," I said to him.

"I know her name," he responded sternly.

"I know you know." I nodded. "But you always refer to her as 'the dog' instead of Cleo."

I sensed the "No I don't" coming, but Papa held back.

"I think if you refer to her by her name instead of 'the dog,' you might actually get to know her better. You might even get to love her."

Papa looked down into his lap. Some of Cleo's white fur had shed onto his black pants and sweater. He shook his head. "I'm not sure you should have brought *Cleo*."

Whatever.

Of course, I actually had no idea how Michael felt about dogs. But I had little choice but to bring Cleo along for the weekend trip since, for the time being, I was her designated caregiver. Candice remained embedded deeply in the last few months of medical school and we had agreed that until she was done, Cleo was best off with me. I was determined to show that I could be relied on, part of my strategy to reassure Candice that her engagement to me was not as much of a gamble as I sometimes sensed she thought it was. In terms of Michael, our friendship had just about hit the ten-year mark and he was now in the same category of many of my other guy friends. I didn't really think much about their preferences or needs. I mean, seriously, what guy did?

Michael's life itself had settled down into a sense of normalcy—at least in the relative sense of his frenzied existence. At the time, he was a dad of two, a boy and a girl to whom he was hopelessly devoted. For the very few that he granted a glimpse inside his private life, they were privy to a doting, deliberate, and disciplined dad. It was clear to those who knew him that Michael had in essence created a family around him to love and be loved in a way that no one else could. He had already overcome one enormous scandal by that time, which, while it never even resulted in formal criminal charges, had severely tainted his image. While still highly respected in many creative circles, he was also regarded by many as freakish, a waning carnival act. Ironically (and perhaps sadly), he was not as sheltered as many believed, and hence very aware of the way that some thought of him. As a result, he had become even more reclusive, convinced that his own kids needed to be protected from the rabid vultures that were so eager to pick apart his celebrity carcass and who he believed would happily gnaw on his kids if given a chance. Getting access into Neverland—itself a shadow of the fantastical home it once was and a place frequented rarely, even by Michael—was uncommon.

If anything, though, Michael still liked to play host to close friends at Neverland. I proudly considered myself among that group. When we arrived at the house late that night and met Michael in the main living room, we exchanged hugs and warm greetings. Then he spied Cleo. "What's that?" he asked suspiciously.

I had kept Cleo on her leash to keep her in check. She was hardly impressed to be meeting the legendary Michael Jackson, and instead was pulling her leash taut in an effort to get me to let her scope out the new digs.

"It's my dog. Her name is Cleo." At the sound of her name Cleo looked up at me. I often said that was her one trick—responding to her name.

"I don't really like dogs." Michael grimaced.

Papa smirked.

"You have a lion. And eat dinner with chimps. How can you not like dogs?"

He laughed.

"Plus—look at her. She's harmless." I ordered Cleo to sit, which required me to actually place my hand on her hips and push them downward. This was not yet in her arsenal of tricks.

"Come here." I gestured to him. Michael inched forward hesitantly. I kept one hand on Cleo's hind and the other now wrenched to her collar. "She's actually very friendly," I lied.

"No she's not," Papa warned.

I shot him a look. "Well, she's not," he said under his breath.

"She reads people really well," I offered. "If you're friendly, she's friendly. If you're, you know, shady and nervous, so is she."

I turned my attention back to Cleo. "Good dog, Cleo . . ." This had become Candice's and my new strategy—positive reenforcement *before* Cleo actually did anything. Generally she did something wrong, so the traditional approach of rewarding her was wayward for us. We were—to say the least—open to new and creative ideas.

I instructed Michael to place his hand in front of her snout so she could smell it. He did so cautiously. "I'm really not into dogs," he reiterated.

Papa sensed a dramatic moment. "Confronting fear with love is the way toward healing."

What he said, I thought to myself.

Meanwhile Cleo was clearly wondering what was up. I could tell by the way her body had tensed under my grasp. She was whimpering too in a way that only I knew was not a harbinger of good things to come. But Michael was already closing in and by the time I tried to jolt Cleo's head away it was too late.

Perhaps sensing Cleo's souring affect, Michael jerked his hand back from her. Seeing this, she reacted predictably by snapping at him with her diminutive jaws. Michael, legendary for being light and agile on his feet, leaped backward, sideswiping a regal piano on which sat a series of portraits. Unsteadied, the portraits clattered and tipped, the first one plummeting toward the ground.

Instinctively I reached out to catch the silver and glass frame to stop it from shattering. But in doing so, I let go of Cleo's leash. Michael froze for a beat, staring at Cleo, realizing now that she was free. Likewise she glared back at him, staring him down and waiting for his next move.

"Don't move," I urged him, slowly putting the picture frame back on the piano. By all accounts, you'd think we were dealing with a runaway tiger. A real possibility at Neverland. But it was too late. Cleo's snarl had spooked Michael. He twitched and Cleo pounced. Michael nimbly dodged her thrust and took off, charging from the living room to the elegant library across the hallway. Undeterred, Cleo ripped right after him, yelping at the top of her lungs.

"Oh shit!" I bellowed, and took off after the pair of them.

"I told you so." Papa shook his head.

AFTER AN ELABORATE RACE through Michael's mansion, I finally came upon the pair in one of the kids' cluttered playrooms.

Cleo had Michael cornered. As a result, he had climbed atop a sturdy wooden table where Cleo couldn't reach him. She, meanwhile, was yapping at him, snapping her small jaws and hopping from side to side with her tail wagging furiously as she waited for him to come down from his perch. She was not trying to scare him, rather was eagerly waiting for them to continue their game of chase. Considering the circumstances and the backstory of Michael's fear of dogs (which I'd later learn), he certainly couldn't be expected to identify the subtle difference in Cleo's intentions, but I most certainly could.

When Cleo intuitively disliked someone, you could see the emotion fully envelop her. When she had bad intentions you could see them almost overtake her entire frame. She stiffened up with anxiety. Her neck and jaw became rigid with suspicion and wariness. She'd plant herself to the ground for stability and snap and growl, making clear her venom. On the other hand, when she felt playful, her body filled up with a very different type of emotion and energy. Her small frame still tensed up rigid and jittered with nervousness, but to me, she looked and felt totally different. Instead of planting herself into the ground, she'd leap from side to side like a welterweight getting ready to spar. Her tail wagged in spasms as if she couldn't wait for what was next. And most notably, instead of the ominous growls and barking, she'd emit what could only be described as a *different* sounding type of growling and barking.

In this case, as Cleo raucously awaited Michael's next move, I knew she was eager for more entertainment. As I tried to scoop her up into my arms, she danced around, agilely eluding my grasp. *What fun*, she must have thought. Everybody is getting in on this wild game.

"It's okay," I reassured Michael. "She just wants to play with you."

He glared at me, terrified. "She's crazy!"

On cue, Cleo backed away, revved her engine, downshifted, and started for the table. About two feet from it, she leaped from her hind legs toward the surface of the table. Michael's eyes widened with a mix of terror and disbelief. He wasn't the only one. Never in her life had I seen Cleo make such an astonishing move. *Maybe*, I wondered, she did know he was the legendary Michael Jackson.

Fortunately for us all, I did manage to harness little Cleo. She wriggled and squirmed in my grasp, craning her neck to kiss and lick my face gleefully.

"See," I told Michael, "she's all excited and happy."

He stared at the pair of us, shaking his head, as if we were aliens. Ironic, I thought, considering his reputation. "Honestly, Michael," I assured him. "Cleo is really harmless. She's just . . . you know . . . different."

Yeah, *different*—that seemed an appropriate description. Or *special*. I shook my head, correcting myself. "She's not like other dogs really. Or any that I know.

"Whatever," I said to Michael as we got back to the library, where my father was waiting for us. "Cleo does things her own way. She lives in her own world." I shrugged. "If it freaks some people out, so be it."

Michael smiled, the first smile in a while. "In that case," he said, "we probably have a lot in common."

ONE OF THE THINGS that Michael and Papa had in common was that they were both serious night owls. Ask my father and he will confess that he spends the hours between ten p.m. and four a.m. switching back and forth between sleep and meditation, occasionally turning on the lights (to my mom's great annoyance) to read a passage in one of the half dozen or so books he keeps stacked beside his bed or make a note (or write a book—I kid you not) into his BlackBerry. Likewise, over the years, whenever I visited Michael, I noticed that often our creative sessions happened in the dead of night. If he wasn't working in those hours, Michael liked to screen old movies, wander around his house, or even go for walks outside in the darkness. Quoting the famous Simon and Garfunkel song, Michael once told me that he preferred the night over the day because it was in the *sound of silence* that he found his own creativity and "heard music."

I myself was never a serious night owl. But the way Michael depicted it as his source of creativity made it sound so attractive that I converted myself into someone who also would wander the darkness in search of inspiration.

To that extent, with the three of us all together—Papa, Michael, and me—this night had the makings of a serious night session. Whereas the relationship between Michael and me had evolved over the years into a pretty familiar friendship, Papa and Michael's was more nuanced. Michael regarded him differently than even many of Papa's other celebrity friends and followers. To him, Papa was not just a friend, and even more than just a teacher and mentor. It wasn't as simple as Papa being a *father figure* to him either, because it ran even deeper than that. I'd learned over the years that *guru* was a dangerous word around Westerners because of all the New Age and woo-woo connotations that it spurred, and yet its true definition was the most accurate way of describing the way in which Michael regarded Papa.

In the Eastern wisdom traditions, not just every student, but every man, woman, and child has a guru. One of my favorite myths growing up was about the great god Lord Rama, who finds himself existentially burdened and wanders into the forest in search of someone to offer him guidance. At one point he comes across an old sage named Vashishta and says he'd like Vashishta to teach him the ways of the world. Vashishta is surprised and laughs. "But you are a god, what can I possibly teach you?"

Rama kneels by the sage's feet and replies, "Even God needs a guru."

There's a devotion, respect, and love unlike any other that defines the relationship between a protégé and his guru. It runs deeper than familial bonds and it transcends that of teacher and student. It's not just the wisdom the guru imparts to his follower, not just words or lessons or insights. Often it's just their being in each other's presence that satisfies them both. Because that's the key— it's a symbiotic relationship. Just like the protégé draws fulfillment from the guru, likewise the guru gets something out of his protégé. Papa had thousands, maybe even millions of followers and fans, and yet he too got something special and totally unique from Michael. It wasn't his celebrity—Papa knew Michael was creatively brilliant, but his was the generation of Elvis and the Beatles and to some extent he believed in Michael's stardom only because I and the rest of popular culture affirmed it to him. It wasn't even Michael's friendship, which was loyal and ironclad. It was in fact a certain elusive quality of trust and respect that bound them.

As much as I loved my father, and as I grew up recognized and respected what he had contributed to the world and the way in which people regarded him for it, I knew in many ways that I would never have the same relationship with him that he and Michael had. My relationship with Papa would always be cluttered by context and circumstance, by the burden of emotion and too much familiarity. Michael and Papa's bond had a purity we could never have. And I was okay with that. In fact, I felt fortunate to just be around it from time to time, playing the third wheel to their holy bond. That night in particular as we settled down in the library, Cleo still eyeing Michael with her tail wagging excitedly and him reciprocating with a slightly less suspicious stare, I sensed we were in for something unusual.

OVER THE YEARS, Cleo had refined the way in which she reacted to anyone outside of family. With very few exceptions she'd barked relentlessly and snarled at *anyone* who came within twenty feet of our house. In the days and weeks that followed Michael's death, as countless television producers, reporters, and an occasional paparazzo showed up outside, Cleo let them have it.

It wasn't such a bad thing. In fact, we figured that Cleo was as good a deterrent as anything. It was next to impossible to conduct a conversation while she yapped and snarled, so I just shrugged and pointed helplessly to my nutty dog. Most got the message and after a few days gave up and called my father's office to get one of us on their shows to talk about our late friend Michael Jackson.

I liked to think that Cleo's ferociousness toward the producers, reporters, and photographers outside the house was in response to the bond that she had built with Michael after their initially dodgy encounter years ago, that her frustration with them and their vulture-like behavior was some sort of loyalty to him. But I knew it wasn't true. Over the last year or so—except in the very rarest of circumstances—she had largely lost her ability to truly differentiate between friendly or unfriendly. Candice and I knew the writing was on the wall. Cleo was an old dog and the fact that she could barely see, smell, or hear anymore had made her generally suspicious and unfriendly toward anyone who didn't take the time to really bond with her. Candice and I didn't talk about it much, but as with most things with Cleo, we were on the same wavelength: It was our responsibility to make her comfortable with her reduced senses and the smaller world that she inhabited as a result. We needed to be the ones to keep her away from situations where she flared and became alarmed or anxious. We needed to be the ones to let her age gracefully, away from the din and madness of the world at large.

As with everything else in the family though, Tara noticed this shift in Cleo and wanted to know what was up. "Why does Cleo bark so much?" she asked over dinner one night. "And at everyone?"

I was trying to figure out how to explain dementia to an eight-year-old when Papa interjected. "Because she's nonjudgmental."

"What does that mean?" Tara asked Papa.

Papa answered, "Cleo treats everyone the same. She doesn't judge people based on whether they are black or white, male or female, friend or foe. She barks at everyone equally—as loud as she possibly can."

Tara laughed along with her grandfather.

That was for sure: Cleo was very much beyond the ordinary duality of the universe. Sinner or saint, divine or diabolical, cowboys or Indians, Republicans or Democrats—she was pretty much a bitch in every sense of the word to all of them. She didn't really differentiate between those that others often polarized, putting at opposite ends of the spectrum so they would be able to make sense of the world around them. Israelis and Palestinians? All the same to Cleo. Hindus and Muslims? Same stock, different day. Leftists and Rightists? Different expressions of the same thing as far as Cleo was concerned. Come one, come all. Everyone got the same response from her: *Woof!*

"We should all see the world like Cleo," Papa pressed on to Tara. "Not judge people because of the names that describe them or the reputations they come with."

Papa took Tara into his lap and spoke to her seriously. "Cleo reacts to people once she gets to know them, based on the way they treat her, not because of what she heard from someone else about them or what she read in a magazine.

"If everyone on the planet treated everyone else like that, we'd probably live in a better, more peaceful world," he concluded.

Tara slid from Papa's lap and walked toward Cleo, who stood by the window still snarling at the unsuspecting pedestrian outside. Tara lowered herself onto a knee and petted Cleo affectionately. "It's okay, Cleo," Tara reassured her.

Tara turned to Mallika. "If we ever get a dog, I hope Cleo teaches it everything she knows."

At that point Candice, Mallika, Sumant, and I shared a knowing glance. We loved Cleo, but she wasn't exactly the mentor type.

"Well, you know . . ." I faded out.

Just then the phone rang. It was a producer for *Larry King Live* requesting either my father or me to come on the show that night to talk more about MJ. That's what it had come to. Take a Chopra, any Chopra, to talk about Michael Jackson. Apparently we drew ratings. Whereas Papa had been fashioned the new sheriff in town, calling to task all physicians who casually prescribed various drugs to patients who helplessly requested them, I had cornered a much softer niche. Not just *son of* anymore, I was now known as the *friend of*, helping to showcase a different side of MJ.

Wait a second, it seemed to have dawned on many all of a sudden—including the countless in the media who had covered Michael's every move for so many years—there was a shred of humanity in the man. In death, finally he had become a real person, not just the inaccessible iconic celluloid celebrity tainted by scandals and weirdness.

I agreed to go on the show. In my own way, I was grateful for the opportunity to bring some relatability to my friend, even in his death. It was my own way of honoring him, helping to shatter some of the judgments that had been made about him. I liked prompting people to question things that they had read or heard about Michael Jackson. I shared stories about Michael as a friend and confidant, as a jokester or opinionated film critic. I talked about what a terrible basketball player he was, but also what a fantastic sketch artist he was. It alternately humanized him and made him more mysterious. He would have liked that.

Later that evening, it happened again at the CNN studio when I made an offhand comment about Michael recently having gotten a puppy for his kids.

"Wait," one of the producers noted during a commercial break, "I thought Michael was afraid of dogs. I swear I read that somewhere."

She probably had. Michael's fear of dogs was well documented, attributed to the fact that his father had had violent fighting dogs when Michael was a kid. He had vividly described some of his memories of just how ferocious they were to Papa and me that night at Neverland years ago. Alas, what hadn't been written about was his change of heart. I'm not going to speculate that Michael ever did get over his fear of dogs, but I can say that he did get a dog—several, if memory serves—over the years for his kids. And I like to think it was that night as well, and Cleo in particular, that had a lasting impression on him and for a brief time turned fear into friendship.

"LET'S MEDITATE," MY FATHER proposed as the four of us—me, him, Cleo (back on her leash), and MJ—sat down on the floor in Michael's Neverland library.

Come again? Papa—you want to meditate? Here, at Neverland?

"Do *meds*"—Michael had a nickname for pretty much everything—"actually work?"

Papa shrugged his shoulders as he crossed his legs and got comfortable. "I don't know. What do you feel when you meditate?"

Michael thought about it for a moment and then confessed: "Most of the time, I just have a lot of thoughts racing through my mind."

"That's okay," Papa reassured him.

"But once in a while" Michael said, "I feel silence."

"Then yes, it's working." Papa smiled at him.

"I like the silence." Michael smiled back at us.

In his case, it was easy to understand why. The silence was out beyond everything. Beyond success and failure. Beyond the love and adulation of celebrity and the need to be relevant and accepted. Beyond the taint of gossip columnists and rumor mongerers.

Cleo seemed resigned to the fact that we weren't going exploring the grounds anytime soon, so she made her customary loops and then plopped down beside me, safely positioned far enough from Michael so she couldn't get at him. He stared at her curiously, reminded of her presence.

"Does she do meds?" he joked.

"She doesn't need to," my father replied. "She lives in the silence."

This time, both Michael and I stared at my father curiously.

Never one to back down from a curious stare, Papa revved up. "Our essential state is one of innocence and infinite possibilities. Cleo isn't influenced by outside factors. She doesn't make judgments of people and situations based on what she's heard around in the neighborhood or read in some blog. She's genuinely curious of the world around her but doesn't carry baggage around with her, uncluttered by memories of the past, free of expectations of the future."

I could tell from Michael's expression that he remained unclear what Papa was saying.

"In other words," I interjected, "she's willing to take you at your word, Michael. She's not relying on what the *National Enquirer* has said about your past and has no secret agenda to impress you and become your best friend. She's not interested in working with you, exploiting you, doing a duet with you, producing your next album, or agenting you."

"And you say she lives in LA? No way," he laughed.

Bittersweet, I thought to myself.

"Nonjudgment is probably one of the most spiritual qualities and the hardest to master," Papa carried on. "Because it forces us to surrender ourselves fully, relinquish the ghosts of our past and the weight of expectations of our futures. To judge people and things spontaneously, even those that we know or have some history with.

"In doing so, we're released from the bonds of our past. Beyond anger and guilt, fearless because we're no longer constricted by the memories of sour experiences and relationships." Papa had his mojo now.

"Heavy stuff." Michael nodded.

Oh, wise Cleo. I ruffled the hair on her head.

"So I don't need to be afraid of the dog?" Michael referenced Cleo, who had rolled over, exposing her belly to me, her signal for me to go to town rubbing it.

"Cleo." Papa smiled, looking at me. "The dog's name is Cleo.

"Most people's fear of dogs is linked to memories of bad experiences in their past," Papa surmised. Quite clearly, the dogs of Michael's past themselves—and the memories of them—were just the gateway to far more tortured memories woven into Michael's conflicted and well-chronicled relationship with his father. That much was clear, even from the little he chose to reveal that night to Papa and me. Such usually is the case with the web of moments that make up our memories.

Michael contemplated all of this for another few moments. "So you are saying that by getting over my fear of dogs, I'd be resolving my past with my father?"

Whoa. Even Deepak dared not go there. "What I am saying, Michael, is that fear of anything can be a toxic emotion and one that can create great challenges in anyone's life.

"It's hard to go into the past and deconstruct it. Not impossible, but very difficult. But the future is different. And like Cleo, we can all choose to be nonjudgmental from this moment forward. To react to things spontaneously and not impose judgments on them before they happen."

"I know what's coming," I interrupted Papa, confident I knew just what was coming.

"Tell him, then." Papa nodded.

"See if you can go a day without complaining, criticizing, or condemning anything. It's harder than it sounds," I qualified for good measure.

This has been one of my father's favorite exercises since I was a kid. It was in fact an exercise in nonjudgment and a very tough one to comply with. Because while prejudging technically meant imposing an opinion, either good or bad, for most people, it almost always meant the latter—i.e., condemning, criticizing, or complaining about something.

"I had dog-fighting growing up in my house," Michael cracked, "and you had this?"

Papa and I burst out laughing.

"Cleo, you said?" Michael stared down at her.

"Yeah." I nodded, unsure by his tone but certain he was about to do something.

He nodded and reached out hesitantly with his hand. Cleo detected it incoming and flipped over from her belly. I held on to her leash, making it rigid once more. Confidently, Michael held his hand beside her snout so she could sniff it, just like I had earlier unsuccessfully instructed him to. Cleo smelled it curiously and then, satisfied that he was friendly, started to lick his hand.

"You can pet her now," I whispered.

And he did. In a few minutes, I had let go of the leash and Cleo moved toward him, snuggling up to his leg. He stared at me unsure what to do and he gestured down toward her. Cautiously, he continued petting her head and neck as she cozied up more to him. It was truly a revelation to all of us—Papa, Michael, and me—as we watched the two of them.

And then Cleo made her move. She flipped onto her back, exposing her belly. This was, of course, her submissive move, a signal that she had fully accepted a new friend and expected to be rewarded for her graciousness She wanted the full rubdown. As she spread her legs and arched her belly upward, Michael's eyes widened in disbelief. This was more than he bargained for.

"Maybe she is an agent after all." Papa laughed.

SITTING IN THE GREENROOM at Larry King's studio, waiting to have our makeup put on, Papa and I watched as a parade of Michael Jackson's friends and colleagues passed through. There was no sign of letup as far as the media coverage was concerned in regard to Michael's death. In fact, in death his legacy was only growing. I myself had already appeared on the show three or four times and my father's presence alongside Larry in the last week or so was at least double that. In many ways we balanced each other. I was able to talk about the times Michael and I snuck into movie theaters just after the opening credits rolled and watched films like *Batman* (one of his favorites). Papa was able to take it further, talking about Michael's existential angst and why Michael claimed to relate so well to a character like the Joker *in Batman*.

By that time, however, even I felt things were petering out. There really wasn't that much more to say, too many more stories to tell. While at first just talking about Michael, recalling some of the stories of the man out of the limelight, made me smile and feel good, a sadness was now setting in. As the stories lost their luster—by that time I had moved onto the B- and C-list ones—the realization only grew that my friend was gone and would not be coming back.

"What are you going to talk about?" I asked Papa, figuring that we should get on the same page so we came across somewhat thoughtful on the broadcast.

"It depends on what he asks, doesn't it?" Papa shrugged, unconcerned.

One thing I had learned in my limited media experience was that in the sound bite media, it actually didn't really matter what the host asked. While someone like Papa may be able to get away with going off script, I liked the idea of wrapping my head around what I wanted to talk about, and pretty much running with it no matter the line of questioning.

"It's not a bad method," Papa remarked when I shared with him my strategy. We both settled into thought for a few minutes.

It was in these moments of reflection though, just sitting and thinking quietly about Michael, that I was getting most down.

"What's wrong?" Papa inquired as I sat there, inertly staring at Dionne Warwick getting her makeup put on.

I shrugged. "Just kind of sad, I guess."

Papa nodded. "Yeah." A beat passed between us. "Let's meditate for a few minutes."

Over the years, meditation had become a panacea in our family. Headache? Meditate. Flu? Meditate. Torn ACL? Meditate. Feeling blue? Meditate. The thing was, it actually worked. For me—a practitioner of meditation from the age of five—almost thirty years later, meditation had become part addiction, part refuge. While I might not be able to articulate the exact science behind it, I was definitely an advocate for it. In college, the only time in my life I ever abused alcohol really, I discovered that meditation was a great remedy for even the worst hangovers. I shared this revelation with a few of my friends and brought them into the cult. (Who says that I have not functionally extended the family legacy?)

To that extent, slipping into meditation in the greenroom at *Larry King Live*, even while the likes of the Reverend Al Sharpton, musician John Mayer, and others meandered about, didn't feel so awkward.

After a few minutes, I opened my eyes and looked at Papa.

As if he sensed me staring at him, he opened his eyes and looked back at me. "What?"

"It's amazing how that actually works." I shook my head. "How does it work?"

"Meditation," Papa responded after a brief pause, "is nonjudgment in action.

"Letting everything spontaneously unfold the way it should. It's listening to the universe without imposing evaluation or qualifications."

"Like Cleo listening to Tara?" I recollected the prior night with a smile.

Papa reciprocated, grinning. "Yeah, actually, exactly like that. You know nonjudgment is not only about not judging people and events? It's emotions as well. It's okay to feel sadness or pain, anger or enmity. Too often people want to find the quick fix. In fact, not only is it okay, it's necessary to emotionally and spiritually evolve to go through proper emotional stages."

It was all getting a little heady for me. I shook my head and asked Papa for a do-over.

Papa nodded. "What I am saying is that we're human *beings*, not human *doings*. Sometime it's okay to just *be*, not worry or judge your feelings. Not have to *do* anything. Just witness your self."

I signaled for him to stop. That was enough for me. "I get it."

Papa smiled, satisfied.

"Okay." He got his game face on and straightened his Liberace glasses. An idea seemed to pop into his head. "Maybe I'll tell the story of our meditation with Michael and Cleo."

PAPA, MICHAEL, CLEO, and I probably meditated for close to twenty minutes that night in the Neverland library.

I remember distinctly when it ended because when I opened my eyes, Michael's were already wide, staring at me.

"What?" I said to him.

"What were you thinking?" he whispered to me.

"I don't know," I said back also in a whisper since Papa still had his eyes shut. "What were you thinking about?" I threw back at him.

"That I need to pee really badly." He smiled.

Papa laughed and opened his eyes. "Then it's definitely working. You better go."

Michael scampered off like a fourth-grader just given permission by his teacher to use the restroom. In a few minutes, he returned looking greatly relieved.

"Why did you say 'it's working'?" he asked as he sat again, warily eyeing Cleo, whose collar I held on to tightly.

Papa responded, "Because when you're doing it right, meditation makes you more alert to everything around you, including whatever you are feeling."

Michael nodded, pleased with himself. He eyed Cleo again. "How old is it?"

"Three-ish," I replied. "*She's* around three."

"How long will she live?"

"Not sure." I shrugged. "Hopefully about fifteen years or so." That's about what I had gathered from various online resources I'd researched.

"Not very long," Michael noted.

"Short and sweet, I guess," I said.

"We are all on death row," Papa interjected dramatically. "The only uncertainty is the length of reprieve and the method of execution."

"Will she get old like humans?" Michael asked.

"Sure." I nodded.

Anyone who has ever had a dog knows the signs. The general fade of the senses—the hearing, sense of smell, sight. I listed them for Michael.

He turned to Papa. "If death came for you right now, would you be ready?"

This was typically Michael, to engage and indulge in the sort of conversations that most did as teenagers at slumber parties. We were now reenacting those missing moments for him.

"All living things age and eventually die," Papa noted, "whether or not you are ready when it comes."

Silence reigned.

✓ "Lord Buddha taught us how to deal with death. It is the great consumer and we are its food."

"Not me." Michael shook his head.

"What does that mean?" I laughed.

"Just that that will never happen to me. Getting old like that. That's all." He shrugged. Looking back, he said it so matter-of-factly that it was unclear how to react. Even my father—so perceptive generally and intuitive on just what to say—seemed a little thrown.

I broke the ominous silence at last. "I'm tired," I announced. "I'm going to go to sleep."

I said my good nights, clutched Cleo's leash tightly, and pulled her away.

As I left, I heard Michael say to Papa, "Buddha, I read about that guy. Tell me his story."

six

What is consciousness?

Really? You expect me to answer that in one go? Every single book I've ever written or that I will write is about consciousness.

Can you sum it up in a paragraph?

Consciousness is the immeasurable potential of all that is, all that was, and all that will be. It is the source of our subjectivity, and also the source of our objectivity. Consciousness simultaneously differentiates into cognition, which is knowing; perception, which is seeing, touching, tasting, and hearing; but it also simultaneously differentiates into behavior, speech, personal relationships, social interactions, our relationship with the environment, and our relationship with the forces of nature. To physicists I would say that consciousness is quantum entanglement, a super-position of possibility waves for space-time events.

Is it time for lunch yet?

It's the wrong question. Lunch relies on whether you're hungry, not what time it is. I live in timeless awareness—I wrote a whole book about it called Ageless Body, Timeless Mind. *If you're physically hungry, sure, let's eat.*

"I'M NOT VERY RELIGIOUS. REALLY MORE SPIRITUAL. . . ." It was a refrain I'd used often in my life. In fact, growing up Chopra, it was a line I'd gotten away with quite a bit. In certain circles—the rarified halls of Columbia, the more New Age blue states, the sound bite–obsessed media—it was actually celebrated as thoughtful and a little provocative. But it didn't really mean anything.

The first part, about not being very religious, was actually true. My parents' religious backgrounds—Hindu and Sikh—never made the migration when they came to the States in the early 1970s. While they weren't exactly pilgrims escaping persecution, traditional religion and all that came with it just wasn't that important to them.

On the other hand, as immigrants without the extensive family they were used to back in the motherland, my parents did value religious culture. How else to imprint their children with a sense of tradition and family? So, while we never really attended temple, participated in religious holidays, or observed the elaborate rituals that often came along with them, we did celebrate our *Indian-ness* in other ways. On Thanksgiving, when most American families were playing football before their turkey dinners, we hung with our Indian friends, played cricket, and ate tandoori chicken. During Easter we'd forgo the chocolate bunnies and have a potluck at our cousins' house, where we'd settle in to watch old Bollywood movies. Only later in life did it become clear to me that my parents were not anti-American, charges I had brought against them in an attempt to get apple pie rather than the sickly sweet Indian desserts that I was used to.

My mother and father were doing their best to help us patch together this new culture we were growing up in. They wanted us to embrace the great American ethos and yet still be grounded by the India that had shaped them. Not something you appreciate as a child, but looking back, I can see what they tried to do, and I can see how.

There was family. Even family that wasn't technically family, like various elders from the community, were referred to as aunts and uncles, and their kids as cousins. It was an expression of the intimacy with which we regarded one another and the familial obligations that came along with it. We might not have lived in India, but my parents and others in the Indian community in and around Boston seemed determined to bring some India to us.

There was food. Appreciating the intricacies of an Indian meal and its many spices—the differences between haldi and jeera, lal mirch and garam masala, and countless others—is in some respects a way of honoring the many textures and subtleties of our cultural homeland. To appreciate the many tastes and flavors of India is to recognize and respect its spectacular diversity. To differentiate how an eggplant is prepared in a northern tandoor compared to how it is marinated and slowly baked in the south is to honor the spectrum of India in all its glory and complexity.

And there were stories. Whether it was the epic myths that chronicled not just the countless gods and goddesses but the great dynasties of eras past, or the lesser known narratives of obscure texts and scriptures, Indian stories and fables were the ones I grew up with. Later in life, I would discover that this was the one real parenting technique that Papa actually consciously and purposefully implemented. It wasn't so much because he wanted us to be Indian, but because he believed the stories resonated deeply and would have a literal effect in shaping us.

"Great myths are not static," he once told me. "They retell themselves over and over in our daily existence. The great heroes and villains of mythic lore are parts of ourselves in embryo and they express themselves over and over again in daily life."

It was standard Joseph Campbell stuff, celebrating the heroes' journey, reminding us there's a reason why certain myths have endured the ages.

"No, it's more than that," Papa insisted. "Reading the greatest stories civilization has ever created is the closest we'll ever come to truly understanding the outer edges of consciousness."

√ *Consciousness.* If Papa's life's work—close to sixty books, not to mention hundreds of blogs, thousands of tweets, and an infinite amount more of assorted insights—could be summarized in one word, *consciousness* would be that word. Consciousness and Papa's dogged exploration of it remained at the core of everything he has written and taught. Even if the vast majority of people never understand it, nor him, Papa is determined to stay the course.

"Yeah, that's probably true," Papa agreed when I proposed it to him on the third hole of the La Costa golf course where he and I were playing. A couple of years earlier, he had become intensely interested in golf—even wrote a best-selling book about it—and I'd gone along for the ride. Expensive clubs and outfits were purchased. Even more expensive classes and courses were identified and played. Stupidly expensive golf vacations were ventured on. As far as Chopra indulgences went, however, golf had been one that captured the attention longer than most. And while in the last year it had waned significantly, we still believed that the game would never truly fade from our lives.

"*Consciousness* is kind of a tough word," I offered.

"Why?" Papa replied as he lined up his putt.

"It's just so, I don't know . . ." I didn't know—that was the problem. "Consciousness is such a big word. It's just so . . . *inclusive.*"

"That's the point." Papa nodded as he tapped his putt. The ball headed straight for the hole and then bled to the right, ending up about four feet wide.

"Consciousness is at the heart of all creation. The source of everything in existence, including us. And it's scientifically provable. It *is* science."

I wasn't convinced, but I didn't really want to engage in a debate either. My mind was veering in a different direction. In recent weeks I had become fixated on how to impart some culture onto my own cut-and-paste kid. It scared me in many ways looking around the neighborhood and culture in which we lived. Aside from it being lily white, it was also not exactly socioeconomically diverse, especially against the greater context of Los Angeles, which is actually one of the most culturally diverse places in the world. The closest these days Krishu was getting to even interacting with people of his own ancestry was Pradeep, the proprietor of the local Indian restaurant, or good old Master Shifu. On the contrary, the only literal stories that Krishu would see in his neighborhood were *Truman Show*–esque. Things were so clean and concise, almost choreographed to sterility. We lived in a culture so supersensitive to political correctness, so organic, so H1N1 paranoid that it made me fear that my boy would never get the dirt beneath his fingernails that I believed was essential to him. And not just in a *kids need to get dirty* way, but in a *how is he going to operate in and contribute meaningfully to the brave new globalized world of the twenty-first century that we all live in?* kind of way. To me, the great Indian myths with which I had grown up, so full of war and conflict between the forces of good and evil, saturated with triumph and treachery amongst the righteous and the nefarious, painted a portrait of a world of contradictions, not just of blacks and whites, but the gray that often loomed in the aftermath. I loved them growing up, read comic books that chronicled them over and over, and sensed at the right time Krishu surely would as well. Still, there were so many stories and fables to choose from. I wanted to make sure that the ones I selected had some purpose to them. It didn't need to be as obvious as "The moral of this story is . . ." and yet I wanted him to know that there was some method behind the madness.

Which myths specifically spoke to consciousness? My father announced that there were only four people in the world who truly understood consciousness. These four were all quantum physicists. I am not a quantum physicist. You do the math. If understanding consciousness were critical, then I lacked confidence that I might select the *right* stories.

I changed tactics. "Is there a word analogous to consciousness that may be easier to wrap one's head around?" I tapped my putt toward the cup, missing it, but not by as much as Papa.

We argued about whose ball was farther from the hole.

"Love," Papa proposed. "How about that?"

It's not a word that I'd have ever guessed. Then again, that explained once more why I was not among the four people in the world who understood consciousness.

As if he'd read my mind, Papa continued, this time invoking one of his favorite poets, the Nobel Prize–winning Rabindranath Tagore. "Love is not a mere sentiment. It is the ultimate force at the heart of creation."

He tapped his ball and watched it disappear into the bottom of the cup. Papa seemed quite satisfied with himself, either because he'd managed a double bogey, a respectful score between the two of us, or maybe because he had crystallized a connection between consciousness and love.

"Find a good myth about unconditional love for Krishu and you'll be on your way," he instructed me.

Well then, I certainly had my marching orders.

BY THE MIDDLE of the summer, several weeks before his birthday, Krishu was gripped by the *terrible twos*. His precociousness and early finesse with languages—English, Spanish, and Mandarin— enabled him to express himself in ways that reflected just how fast his mind was developing.

"*Quiero huevos con queso,*" he chirped when we rolled into the kitchen between showings of *Kung Fu Panda*.

"*Huàn niaòbù?*" he'd announce, alerting us in Mandarin that his diaper needed to be changed.

But it was one early morning when he awoke between Candice and me that he made his most dramatic announcement: "I want to fight Cleo." We stared at him, unsure how to react. He said it with such clarity and precision, as if it was a decision he'd spent considerable time pondering and debating internally. We didn't know whether to be humored by it or troubled.

In fact, it was evidence of a growing trend we'd started to see over the last few months. Often, I'd find him gathering whatever was within reach—pillows on the couch, books off the shelves, food from the tables—and firing it directly at Cleo's head. Still somewhat spry and agile, not to mention wise to Krishu's increasingly shady ways, Cleo knew how to dodge her opponent's advances. She'd leap from her perch wherever she was and scurry away to the safe zones she'd located around the house: beneath the kitchen table, behind the couch, up atop the elevated bed in the guest room. Still, Krishu was relentless. When Cleo's guard was down, he'd commandeer one of his toys—a dump truck, its trailer full of oversized

LEGO pieces—and chase her around the room. Occasionally he'd clip her leg with the plastic truck, or if he was strategic enough, corner her and then commence the heavy artillery fire with the oversized LEGOs.

The most elaborate and disturbing scheme he'd concocted was, ironically, short of physical aggression. Krishu would squeeze himself behind the couch, running his hands through the significant dust balls that had settled there, and place them squarely in Cleo's water bowl, presumably to contaminate it and render it undrinkable. It was truly diabolical in nature, evidence of an advanced level of calculated deviousness in the league of supervillains like Lex Luthor or the Joker. I didn't know whether to be impressed or afraid.

Whatever the case, Krishu's declaration that he wanted to fight Cleo couldn't simply be shrugged off. It wasn't just something he'd figured out how to say; he was willing to back it up in action. And it was aligned with other milestones too. Recently he'd become very defiant, refusing to eat at mealtimes, demanding television and/or candy, usually accompanied with the screaming qualifier "now," just to ensure we were aware of how pressing his desires were. The teachers at his preschool where he went once a week for "structured play" (whatever that was) reassured us that Krishu was simply "feeling out his boundaries." They warned us that the process could last a while, until Krishu got a good grasp of exactly how far he could push us as parents or test out which techniques worked on us. Only then, when the rules and boundaries had been established, would he settle down and we'd all find our comfort zone.

Comfort zone, my . . .

The most important thing, our confidants advised us, was to be consistent. Krishu was looking for signals from us, to establish limits, and we had to reciprocate. "The one thing you can control," a child psychologist friend of Candice's counseled her, "is how you respond to him. *Own what you control.*" ✓

That last line—*own what you control*—felt decidedly Vince Lombardi. It sounded so rigid and premeditated, so out of a parenting coaching manual and devoid of the *au naturale* parenting technique I liked to claim was more my style. But the fact that Krishu was feeling out his boundaries by trying to assassinate Cleo could not be denied nor ignored. It demanded action. I had no choice but to *own it*, whatever *it* was.

When I recounted all of this to Papa somewhere along the sixth hole, he nodded in contemplation as if noodling the answer to an elaborate calculus problem. We'd already established that I needed a great myth about unconditional love—and I was on it—but now I wanted more precise and immediate advice.

This was generally the type of predicament that I'd bring to my mother, but she wasn't available. Mallika was second in line, but she had made it clear that her experience with two thoughtful, nurturing girls did not lend itself to what we were dealing with with Krishu. Beyond all of that, in recent weeks my relationship with my father had evolved considerably. We'd talked about things, both mundane and mystical, more than any time I could really remember. We'd become closer, not just as father and son, student and teacher, but even as friends. Now in many ways the fact that he was the least likely person to go to (for me) for parenting advice made the mere prospect of it intriguing. What was there to lose—I mean, really?

"How does Cleo respond to Krishu?" he asked as he lined up his drive on the seventh tee.

Occasionally she'd growl pathetically or flash her tiny incisors at him, but that was pretty much the extent of it. Generally she was adept at dodging him, even as he evolved his techniques. And by and large, she didn't even adapt her own behavior. In other words, after she'd managed to elude his latest foray and Krishu had lost his will or placed his attention elsewhere, Cleo eventually reverted to normal. She'd usually go back to sitting in the same location, placing herself once more in his crosshairs, where he'd eventually notice her and his scheming would start anew.

"Either she's just really stupid . . ." I shrugged.

"Or she's incredibly loyal," Papa interjected, and with that, he swung his club and smacked the ball, sending it straight down the expansive fairway. We both watched it roll down the grass with a mix of admiration and surprise.

"I think it's the latter," he concluded when the ball finally came to a rest. "Tell me more about how she is around him."

All observation suggested that Cleo was hopelessly devoted to Krishu. She followed him around wherever he went. At first Candice and I believed that it was because he always had food hanging around him, off him, or on him. But then again, her affection for him preceded his arrival into the world of real food. The day we brought Krishu home from the hospital, Cleo inspected him curiously. What was this? Could she eat him? (Her first question with everything.) When was he leaving? (Her second question.) Once Cleo figured out that he was in the house to stay, she seemed to form a bond with Krishu.

The baby seemed to be the first thing that interested Cleo for longer than the time it took to down a Greenie. And why not? He was her size, after all. He often had a rank odor, which appeared to be a major turn-on for her. And his mood was unpredictable, which kept all of us on our toes. In anticipation of this reconfigured household, I had read a few books (okay, blogs) that suggested that dogs often saw children not necessarily as humans, but as just another part of the pack. And because of their diminutive statures, they often perceived children as competitors for their place in that pack. While Cleo went through her own phase of intrigue around Krishu, trying to figure out how he was going to fit into our previously tight unit, she never appeared to form any resentment toward him, nothing, really, to suggest that she thought of him as competition.

Okay, I knew I was anthropomorphizing Cleo, that I was subjecting her to my own human thought process. If I had learned anything from watching her through the years, it was that she walked to the beat of her own drum. And that drum was more of a banjo. Still, there were things that were just plain to see. At night, we would often lay Krishu to sleep on a bed in his playroom. The vast majority of the time, Candice was the one who managed this process with an elaborate routine involving music and reading and other rituals that only she and Krishu were privy to. During this time, Cleo and I were remanded mostly to the living room. It was my time to watch baseball or basketball games or surf the Internet. Whereas prior to Krishu's arrival into the house, I could almost always count on Cleo to sit by my side while I indulged in these activities, now her priorities had changed.

Instead of sitting with me, she'd position herself outside of Krishu's door, find her spot on the wooden floor, and hunker down. Usually after about an hour, the door would open and as Candice emerged, Cleo would salute her with a brush along her leg as she passed into Krishu's room. She'd glance upward with a seeming wink and a nod, an *I'll take it from here.*

At first Candice and I paid close attention to this routine, curious ourselves as to what Cleo was doing and also to ensure that indeed she didn't have any intentions to eat the boy. It all seemed innocent enough. Cleo's routine generally consisted of a sniff and a lick of Krishu's crown, followed by her measuring out a safe distance from his legs, where she'd again do her loops before settling down in a heap.

At the risk of sounding overly sentimental, I'll confess that this was one of the most treasured sights Candice and I ever witnessed. If you watched her closely—and as youngish parents with not much else to do, we did indeed often watch Krishu and Cleo as if they were ranging in a wild animal park—Cleo would initially keep her eyes open for some time and just stare at Krishu as he breathed deeply in and out. Of course, it wasn't entirely clear what she was thinking in these quiet moments, but Candice and I speculated that it was roughly what we did when we gazed lovingly at our son— that we really, truly loved him . . . and were so damn relieved that he was finally asleep.

When Krishu arrived in our world, he ignited a powerful love in me that I never knew existed. And on those nights, after Krishu and Cleo had gone to sleep, I'd think to myself just how funny it was that many of the clichés I'd heard about having a child were so accurate.

"You can't imagine how much you'll love them," countless friends with kids had told us before we had our own. "Every day gets better," they'd say with wide smiles. Blah, blah, blah. I'd told Candice while she was pregnant and we had to endure these self-obsessive confessions that we'd never be those people. For some reason I found their unsolicited declarations of love annoying. However, in the privacy of my home, observing my kid and my dog, I was entitled to think along whatever clichés I wanted. Even if I couldn't fully articulate it, I knew that the love I had for my son was unconditional.

"So." Papa tapped his putter on the ground as we arrived at a rest stop where we'd share a big bag of peanuts. "What you're saying is that Cleo's love of Krishu is special."

"Sure." I nodded. *Special* was a broad description, but it felt appropriate.

"What I mean," Papa added, "is that her love for him is made up of qualities like forgiveness, patience, grace, devotion, compassion, empathy, and nonjudgment."

That certainly was a lot more than *special*. I mulled the words and nodded. They seemed to fit the bill.

For all of his countless daily attacks on her, Cleo never held a grudge against Krishu. To that extent, she certainly was forgiving.

The way she hovered around him, watching over him especially when he slept, demonstrated a degree of grace that was enviable as well.

Devotion?

Check.

Compassion and empathy?

Indeed. All you had to do was witness the few times when Krishu was reprimanded for doing something bad. Sad-faced, he'd retreat to his playroom for "quiet time" and Cleo, his comrade in arms, would loyally trail him.

Nonjudgment?

See chapter 5.

"Well," Papa concluded as if he'd heard the symptoms and had a diagnosis, "that's unconditional love.

"Cleo's devotion to Krishu does not rely on anything other than the bond she has formed with him. Her love for him is timeless and anxiety-free. It's not grounded in expectations of reciprocity or paranoia about who loves whom more. Presumably she doesn't worry about the future of their relationship or analyze its history and hold grudges for past transgressions.

"She loves Krishu because of who he is, not because of her idea of him. She loves him the way he is, not for the way she wants him to be."

Papa laughed. "It's very nonhuman, the more you think about it. Relationships between humans and their love of one another are frequently more conditional and fleeting."

Anyone who's ever been *in love* absolutely knows this to be true. Love can be passionate and deep, intense in its application and romance, but rarely, if ever, is it unconditional. It's just not the way we seem to be wired.

"Sure," Papa agreed with me as we finished off our peanuts and wandered toward the next tee. "But that doesn't mean we shouldn't aspire toward an ideal, to seek unconditional love.

"In fact," he said as he reached for his driver and pulled it from his golf bag, "learning how to love one another unconditionally, like Cleo does, can take us to higher states of consciousness."

BEFORE KRISHU CAME along and shot his arrow through Cleo's heart, she was almost exclusively devoted to Candice and me. And within that love triangle, despite my best efforts, I knew to Cleo I'd forever remain Candice's sidekick. They had a special bond. Cleo was more than Candice's once puppy, a little ball of fur that fit in the palm of her hand. She was even more than just the clichéd best friend. Cleo was Candice's companion in a way that even I, who had known Candice from the time we were both college kids, never really could be. It was because of her ability to listen and not judge, the joy and innocence she brought to every day, her ability to trust, and more. But most of all, it was her unconditional love.

And even though she played favorites, visibly ranking Candice higher on the chart than me, Cleo had a unique ability to navigate the sometimes tricky terrain of our relationship even in its most intense and rankled moments. This was perhaps no more evident than on the night before our wedding.

As part of our multicultural Chinese-Indian-American wedding celebration, Candice and I had planned a weekend's worth of activities that included a cocktail party in a quasi-kama-sutra-like lounge, a traditional Chinese banquet, a midmorning Sikh-styled wedding ceremony, all of which would culminate in a blow-out party/reception in a Unity church on Manhattan's Upper West Side. All in all, we had roughly 450 guests flooding into the city, an intimate gathering by Asian wedding standards.

Somehow, though, amidst all of this madness, with family in town from all the four corners of the globe and shacked up in various hotels and relatives' and friends' homes, I managed to find myself staying all alone in my midtown apartment. Candice, meanwhile, had moved her wedding wardrobe to stay with family in their hotel. Out of respect to whatever traditions had managed to penetrate our nontraditional wedding weekend, Candice and I hardly saw much of each other except during the formal events. Considering all of this, we had determined that Cleo was best off staying with me during the chaos.

In the midst of all of these activities and obligations—not to mention the momentous specter of entering into marriage and all of its *for better and for worse* implications—I found myself greatly comforted by Cleo's presence. In the week leading up to the wedding, I often found that when I returned from late night last calls of bachelorhood with my friends, I was unable to drift into sleep. Instead, I'd lounge on the couch, the most expensive thing I'd ever purchased in my life prior to Candice's engagement ring, with Cleo draped over me. Together we'd watch SportsCenter or old movies.

As the wedding day drew closer, our bond intensified. In recent years Candice had become the person to whom I expressed my hopes and fears, dreams and trepidations. Now, not only was I restricted from seeing her, but she was also the source and object of those emotions. Cleo, on the other hand, was free and available, her calendar completely devoid of any other commitments. She was willing to indulge my confessions and anxieties, especially if they were accompanied by bagels, pizza crust, deli meats, or the other late night munchies I brought home. The night of the prewedding Chinese dinner banquet would require all of her skillful listening and more.

Banquet meals are traditional affairs in Chinese culture. As in Indian culture, food is not just a way of demonstrating a family's prosperity, but the more diversity of it, the greater the celebration. Candice's family had organized a gala affair, packed with multiple courses, an open bar, and lots of extended family. While everyone had a splendid time, indulging in shark fin soup, crab dumplings, and more, Candice and I carried out our duty, shuffling from one table to the next, welcoming extended family members we hardly knew who had come to bless us with their presence.

It was a "grin and bear it" affair from beginning to end. For Candice, this effect was literal; she was squeezed tightly into a traditional Chinese chi pao. I had joked with her leading up to our wedding that, like a good Chinese bride, she had spent months shedding pounds (and by all appearances a few ribs as well) to get into that dress. Her restricted gait—she shuffled slowly from one table to the next—made her wince every step of the way. My feigned disposition could really only be attributed to the fact that I just plain disliked, and was no good at, being social. There was only one way I was going to parade around for hours in front of family members I didn't recognize and indulge in conversations about things I didn't care about: alcohol.

As we moved around the banquet hall I kept a bottle of Tsingtao beer in my palm, nursing it slowly between winks, nods, hand-shaking, and fake laughs. Sprinkled between gulps of beer came toasts with jolts of a concentrated rice wine. By the end of our seemingly endless greeting parade, Candice could hardly stand because her dress was so tight. I could hardly stand because I was so drunk.

"Bro, you may want to slow down on the booze," one of my friends advised me as I staggered to keep my balance. "You're getting married tomorrow after all."

"No, bro," Candice's brother ominously countered as he poured another shot of rice wine, "if I were you, I'd drink more. After all you're getting married to my sister tomorrow."

Still, further solidifying that I'd truly found my soul mate in Candice, she managed to pull me aside and confide that she'd thought up an exit plan to get us out of the dinner. Was this girl great, or what? We weren't even married yet and she was already greasing the wheels for me to slip out of cumbersome family obligations. She went over the plan. We were skipping out on our own banquet in order to get ready for the big day tomorrow. Remarkably, amidst this elaborate banquet affair, Candice had been able to hatch the perfect plan and she now confided it to me.

If only my elevated blood alcohol had not gotten in the way of my seeing straight and hearing clearly. If so, I'd have understood that the plan included our leaving the banquet *together.* Not me leaving my bride-to-be on the street corner. In the rain. In her tight-fitting chi pao. With no money.

By the time I reached home, I had multiple messages summoning me to the hotel where Candice was staying. My bride wanted to see me. That was all.

Still none the wiser, my only warning came from Candice's soft-spoken mother. "Be careful," she whispered as I entered their room.

Over the course of the next twenty minutes, the floodgates opened and the emotions poured out.

How could I possibly have just left her on the side of the road?

What was I thinking?

How much had I drunk?

Was this a sign of things to come?

Did I even love her?

I stumbled and mumbled. Stammered while hammered and struggled my way through admissions, apologies, denials, deflections, defenses, promises, and pledges. Was it simply an inebriated transgression, Candice wanted to know, or a pattern of behavior, intimating a lack of readiness to truly take on the obligations and responsibilities of marriage?

Whoa. A lifeline perhaps? Nope—not even my charm and wit would save my ass this night. Soon Candice sent me on my weary way, instructing me to think about it overnight, if I was really ready for the plunge we were about to take.

I retreated back to my apartment with the full intention of collapsing onto the couch, where I planned to spend the whole night feeling sorry for myself. Alas, I had forgotten about Cleo, who'd by then been cooped up in the apartment, going on about ten hours. Even as I ached to take a load off and wallow in self-pity, Cleo made herself clear, lurching from side to side, pawing at my pants legs, and snarling. She needed to go out.

I changed from my suit into sweats and rummaged through the closet to find a pair of sneakers. Seeing this transformation, Cleo's snarls changed to excited yaps, and she pranced around the room, knowing this ritual ended with us going for a walk. No matter what frayed emotions I was struggling with, at that moment Cleo's focus and attention was singular: She needed to go out and it was up to me to make it happen.

As was our usual routine, I'd planned to take her for a quick loop around the block and quickly hustle back upstairs, where I could get back to my solitary pity party. But as we came to the third turn that would start the procession home, Cleo dug her heels in. Literally. She yanked her neck, and gestured as if she wanted to keep going.

"Come on, Cleo," I urged her. "Let's go home." I dashed a little enthusiasm into my voice as if suggesting that perhaps a treat awaited us back at the ranch.

No dice. Cleo jerked harder, pulling her leash toward downtown. *Yeah right,* I'm sure she was thinking to herself, *let's go back to your messy bachelor pad so I can watch you cry yourself to sleep. No thanks. I'm not that much of a sucker for a Greenie.*

This time she barked and pulled even harder.

Fine, I relented, letting her pull me westward. I could hold out another block.

As we walked, we came upon the corner of Fifty-fourth Street and Broadway. Cleo stopped to sniff something on the sidewalk and I waited. I looked up to find myself facing a wall of large maroon posters for the show *Miss Saigon*. Staring at them, I smiled, remembering the last time I stood in that exact spot.

Miss Saigon had been one of the first Broadway shows Candice and I had ever seen together. A simpleton when it came to theater, I'd of course enjoyed it, chiefly because the star was a sexy Asian girl and the story hit all the formulaic dramatic beats with considerable pomp and pageantry. Candice, on the other hand, found it, well, formulaic, not to mention saturated with all of the Orientalist stereotypes that canonized Western masculinity while dispiriting the East.

I shrugged, unconvinced. "John [the ex-soldier turned executive] tried to do her right . . ."

Candice turned to me, irritated. "Oh, is that what you're doing with me? Doing me right?"

I laughed out loud at the recollection. Cleo jerked her leash again, this time pulling me downtown. Maybe she knew what she was doing, I thought to myself, and followed her lead.

Indeed, over the course of the next few hours, I let Cleo lead the way, guiding me from midtown Manhattan all the way to lower Manhattan and the Wall Street area. It was a tour through Candice's and my history together. Fiftieth and Broadway, the pommes frites booth where we shared a last supper (a bucket of frites with tartar sauce) the night before I moved to California. The TKTS discount ticket booth in Times Square where we had spent many an hour waiting in long lines to purchase tickets so Candice could educate me on *good* Broadway shows. Madison Square Garden, where I took Candice to her first NBA game (Celtics-Knicks circa 1996) and I defended her honor when an Asian punk wearing a John Starks jersey made a lewd comment toward her. Thirty-third and Seventh, Koreatown, to this day our favorite spot for a great meal. Chinatown, where through the years she'd flaunted her Mandarin and earned us special dishes not on the menu. And finally Ground Zero, the former World Trade Center site, a monument to a moment, that like every other American vaguely associated with it, bound us together in our shared panic, disbelief, and subsequent grief.

By the end of our long walk, Cleo had not only sobered me up, but had reminded me why I was in fact ready for my wedding day. Sure, a part of me was scared by the thought of marriage. Candice was the first and last serious commitment I'd ever made to anyone, the only adult relationship I'd ever really been in. While I often told people that she and I had essentially grown up together, part of me wondered if we had grown up at all. Still, something deep inside me, some strong sense of self convinced me I was on the right path. Looking down at my weary loyal dog, I knew I had a companion on that journey in Cleo. I picked her up, kissed her dusty nose, and flagged down a cab. It was time to go home. Cleo's love and loyalty was affectionate without being patronizing. Empathetic without being untrue. Regenerative, nurturing, and intense without being fleeting. I realized then and I realize now writing this that all of these observations were my own projections. In reality, Cleo's behavior patterns were simple and predictable and for the most part reliant on a single discernable, though eminently powerful, characteristic: She *gives* love.

BACK ON THE GOLF course, Papa made it a point to single this out. "When we talk about the power of love, its therapeutic and regenerative effects, we're almost always referring to what it's like to be the object or recipient of someone's love.

"But it's even more powerful when you are the one doing the loving. There's a purity to that love, the way a child loves its parent early on and vice versa. It's unfiltered, naked, stripped of the burdens of time, context, and conditions. It's everything you've described about Cleo."

Over the course of the last few weeks, Papa had spent more time with Cleo than he ever had before. He was observing and studying things in her he'd never even noticed.

"Do you think Cleo truly understands the concept of love?" I posed to Papa, thinking maybe we were going a little overboard here.

"No, and that's what makes it so powerful.

"There's a playfulness and grace to the way in which Cleo reacts to those she loves. She trusts us with a sense of transcendence.

There are no gradients to that, no measure to how or how much she loves. She's unobtrusive with her attention. It's not dependent on your behavior. With those she loves, she does so simply because they are."

"I FOUND IT," I told Papa a week later when he was again in LA, staying with us. We were sitting in the living room late at night. Krishu was asleep in his room, while Candice was reading manga comics online, her favorite pastime.

"Found what?"

"The story. On love—unconditional love." I nodded. "It's from the Mahabharata about the Pandava brothers."

Papa looked at me, intrigued. "Tell it to me."

Growing up, the stories of the Mahabharata, one of India's epic and most seminal narratives (akin to the Iliad or the Odyssey in the West), had been my favorite. The whole saga is a sprawling narrative that chronicles the feud between the five righteous Pandava brothers and their nefarious rival cousins, the one hundred Kaurava brothers. At the heart of the story is an eighteen-day battle waged between the two sides, pitting a single—albeit expansive—family against one another. Brothers, fathers, sons, uncles, mentors, protégés, gods, and demigods all engaged in a single mythic and gruesome war, the outcome of which will determine the fate of the cosmos.

In the end, of course, the noble Pandava brothers triumph, having slaughtered all their rivals as well as having suffered massive casualties on their own side. As a consequence, though, in the aftermath of so much violence and loss, they question what they have really earned in victory. Faced with this existential dilemma that they cannot really resolve, the brothers relinquish the hard-fought kingdom they've gained to their last living heir—a single nephew who has survived the war—and set off for the mythic realm of Kailash (the threshold to the heavens) in search of God's blessings.

The five brothers, led by the eldest, Yudishtra, and their consort, Draupadi, set forth for the arduous ascent upward. Early on, in one of the poor villages at the base of the mountains, a mangy dog straggles behind the group, following them on their pilgrimage.

But as they ascend the mountainside and the climb gets more challenging, bad things happen. The youngest brother, Nakula, slips on some ice and falls over the ledge, plunging to his death. After mourning the loss of their brother, the brothers continue upward in pursuit of their literal lofty goal.

Now the shit really hits the fan, because as the group and mangy dog continue their ascent, like in some B-list horror flick, one by one the brothers and even Draupadi slip and fall to their deaths. Only Yudishtra and the dog survive and reach the mountain's apex.

It's here that Yudishtra encounters Indra, king of the gods and the heavens. He congratulates Yudishtra on successfully completing the climb and says he's earned himself a spot in the kingdom of heaven. He opens the door to his divine chariot and invites Yudishtra in for the short ride toward eternal bliss. Yudishtra thanks him and makes his move for the chariot, gesturing to the mangy dog to follow him.

But wait!

Indra blocks the dog and informs Yudishtra that dogs—certainly dirty village ones—are not welcome in heaven. Yudishtra halts and says that the loyal dog has stayed by his side the entire ascent and he has no intention of abandoning his loyal companion at this point.

Indra appears flummoxed and irritated. Yudishtra is willing to abandon his own brothers and Draupadi during the ascent but not this dirty dog, even now that he is being granted entrance into heaven?

Yudishtra shakes his head solemnly. He explains that he did not leave his brothers nor Draupadi. They were taken from him, and he presumes it was so because of some divine plan that he's not privy to. He insists that he has faith that he will be reunited with his loved ones when the time is right. With that, he reiterates his unwillingness to proceed if the dog is not by his side.

Lord Indra breaks into a wide smile at last. Suddenly the dog itself begins to transform and is revealed as the god Dharma, which is none other than an incarnation of Indra himself. Welcome to the Matrix! He explains that the whole episode from the journey up the hill, to the death of Yudishtra's loved ones, to the offer to escort Yudishtra to the heavens *sans* the dog was all a test. And Yudishtra has passed with flying colors. Now, together Yudishtra, Lord Indra, and Lord Dharma enter the heavens, where eventually Yudishtra will be reunited with his brothers and Draupadi.

After relaying the story to Papa, I sat back on the couch, pleased with myself. He nodded, seemingly equally delighted.

"It's a good story," he noted.

"I know. It's a great story."

"What do you think it means?" he asked.

"Well, a lot of things." I gestured with my hands. "Where to start, really?"

"With the ending," Papa replied. "The dog is Dharma and Dharma is the self. The idea of loving one's self in the West has a bad connotation. It's the difference between the god Dharma in the East and Narcissus in the West."

Sure enough in Greek mythology, Narcissus is a hero renowned for his exceeding beauty. But he's cruel and spurns all who love him. As such, he's eventually cursed by the other gods, forced to fall in love with his own beauty and, like all those suitors whom he despised, he now hates his own self.

"Right." Papa nodded. "But in the Eastern traditions, the *self* is everything. It is behind your thoughts, the very same force that is responsible for all the intelligent activity of the universe including the dog."

"It is consciousness," I interjected.

"Yes." Papa laughed. "Not bad."

"So can we say that there are now five people in the world who understand consciousness?" I asked Papa, grinning.

"Maybe," he conceded.

"So what you are saying is that the dog is a metaphor for the self, which is just another expression for consciousness?"

Both Papa and I looked at Cleo, who lay outside Krishu's door in a light sleep. She underplayed her role as cosmic seer remarkably well.

"I don't think it's any coincidence." Papa shook his head.

"The great seers of India who wrote these stories must have known—dogs are *spiritual* beings."

seven

Papa, I'm wondering why bad things happen to good people.
Bad things happen to everyone.

ON JANUARY 20, 2001, MY PATERNAL GRANDFATHER—WE called him Daddy—sat in his bedroom in New Delhi watching the inauguration of George W. Bush on CNN. Daddy was a student of history and he enjoyed playing witness to moments like these. More than fifty years ago he had had a front row seat to India's dramatic transition. From the grip of British colonialism, to the euphoria of independence, to the agony of partition between India and the newly created Pakistan, he was eyewitness to it all. Daddy was the personal physician to Lord Mountbatten—the last Viceroy of India—so he had an intimacy with and insight into the highest levels of the British Raj and its rule over his country. Growing up I would sit with rapt attention as he told stories of his years of service in the Indian army—stories about the siege of

Burma, when he became the only surviving member of his military unit by playing dead and eluding his Japanese would-be captors; historic journeys alongside Lord Mountbatten; proud tales about the time when India's iconic hero and first prime minister post-independence, Jawaharlal Nehru, stopped amidst a sea of admirers to hand our grandmother a red rose.

Daddy sat in his bedroom that night amidst a tangled testament to all of that history. Portraits of my grandmother Ma were proudly displayed alongside Daddy's regal days with British colleagues during his posts all around India, not to mention London, where he had done much of his medical training. There were more recent pictures too, updated photographs of Daddy and Ma beaming with their five grandchildren. Only three weeks earlier, we'd all celebrated the marriage of my younger cousin, Kanika. It had been a classic Indian extravaganza, packed with decadent parties, religious rituals, and endless family affairs. Hundreds of pictures captured those wondrous days, but had yet to find their way into any frames. Instead they lay in stacks, tucked into envelopes, piled on the wooden chest that stood just beyond Ma and Daddy's bed.

After watching President Bush take his oath on that rainy day in Washington, DC, and officially accept the duty and responsibility of the presidency—qualities that Daddy held in the highest esteem—he settled into bed beside Ma, who was already fast asleep. Rarely in their fifty-four years of marriage had they slept apart. Shortly after midnight, Daddy rang the bell beside the bed to call Shanti, the family servant for more than twenty-five years. When Shanti showed up a few minutes later, Daddy said he felt cold and needed a blanket for the night. Daddy returned to sleep. Not long afterward, he awoke again. This time Daddy sat up and felt his chest. He was one of India's most well-respected cardiologists and was still practicing well into his seventies. He knew what was happening. Daddy reached for Ma and rustled her from her sleep. She too sat up and asked him what was wrong. Daddy informed her that he was dying. Ma panicked and reached for the phone to dial my uncle, a physician who lived not too far away. Daddy, still clutching his chest, told Ma to put the phone down. There wasn't much time left, he explained.

"Just hold my hand," he instructed her. And she listened. Ma and Daddy held hands as he took his last breaths. "I love you," he told her softly, "and I am leaving."

Daddy closed his eyes a final time, embracing the mystery of death. "I am leaving."

THE LOGISTICS OF DEATH came fast and furious. Family arrangements, overseas travel, death certificates, and Hindu rituals overwhelmed. By morning, Hindu priests were summoned to the house to perform chants, bless Daddy's body, his home, and Ma to ensure a smooth transition to the next phase of his soul's evolution. By religious mandate, Daddy's cremation ceremony had to take place within thirty hours of death. My father and his brother, Chota Papa, made it just in time. The two of them bathed Daddy's body with milk, anointed it with sandal oil, and carried it on their shoulders for the last hundred yards to the cremation site. Papa, the older son, placed a torch beneath the funeral pyre, igniting it so Daddy's body could return to the elements from where it came.

Later when I spoke to my father, he'd describe to me the emotional odyssey he'd been on the last two days.

"You know, someday you too will burn my body," he said over the crackly long-distance line. "It'll be your responsibility as my son. And someday far in the future, your unborn son will do the same to you."

I wasn't sure how to respond. The thought was creepy, solemn, sci-fi, and spiritual all at the same time.

"They say it's one generation allowing another to pass to the next phase," Papa said.

"It must have been difficult," I said softly. I knew that Papa admired his father like no one else in his life. I'd never in my life heard him speak critically about Daddy.

"It was." Papa paused. "But I'm glad I did it. It's a privilege."

Papa described the hymns the Vedic priests chanted during the ceremony, about the tangled web of *agni* (fire), *vayu* (wind), *paani* (water), *dharti* (Earth), and their inevitable return to the imperishable *akash* (space).

"It's all we are, really," Papa surmised, "a cluster of the elements, ignited by some energy and a deeper mystery. And we're all destined to fade back into an even greater mystery at the end."

Papa even laughed as he narrated how as the priests chanted those hymns, a few hundred yards away young boys played cricket, and farther along, still younger boys flew their kites using the draft of the fire to lift their kites high into the sky. Nearby, Scottish bagpipes mingled with gaudy blaring Hindi film music, indicating that a wedding was going on in the neighborhood. Meanwhile, the priests continued to chant, speaking of the immortality of the human soul. "Water cannot wet it, wind cannot dry it, fire cannot burn it, weapons cannot shatter it. It is unborn, beyond space and time, and does not die."

The full impact of Daddy's death would not hit home for Papa until weeks later, when he had returned to his home—to us—in America. It was in those days as the residue of death lingered that our memories of Daddy started to organize themselves in the archives of our minds.

Over dinner one night when the whole family had assembled in

San Diego, Mallika recalled a scene from Kanika's wedding just weeks before. Early in the morning of the wedding itself, the whole family had gone through a major crisis. My aunt—Kanika's mother—had misplaced the key to the room where Kanika's expensive jewelry and bridal dress had been very carefully stored. There were just a few hours left before the ceremony and poor Kanika was distraught because her worst fears were coming true. What would she wear?

In the chaos, everyone searched for the missing key. Tempers flared. There was a lot of finger pointing and blaming. I did my best James Bond impersonation, slipping a credit card in the crack of the door hoping it would unlock. No luck. My younger cousin Bharat threw himself at the door with all his weight—nothing happened.

Suddenly we saw Daddy ambling up the stairs, deliberate and slow. He held a ring of keys in his hands. None of them were the "right ones," just standard keys for other doors and safes in the house. But that didn't bother Daddy, nor deter him. While we frantically searched here and there like an unskilled forensic team emptying purses, pulling blankets off beds, and rummaging through the pockets of clothes, Daddy bent over, peering at the lock carefully. I tried to explain to him that the door would not open unless we found the right key.

He smiled and said softly with conviction, "No, it will open."

Meanwhile my uncle—Kanika's father—expressed his indignation and anger over what he observed had been a perennial theme for the past fifteen years, the key being locked inside the room. Daddy remarked that the locksmith—a fellow named Vinod— never showed up when they called in emergencies like this. But Daddy knew what to do. He quietly explained that if you played with the lock, wriggled the key in a certain manner, and pulled the door in a certain other manner, it would open.

Sure enough a few minutes later the door gently opened. Daddy smiled pleasantly and quietly shuffled back to his room.

Everyone grew quiet and we shared an unspoken admiration for the quiet, loving soul who was our grandfather. We knew in that moment—and we were reminded of it at dinner—something we had known since we were little children: Daddy was an opener of doors.

Papa smiled, his eyes misty. It was the first of a chain of emotional moments strung over the next few months. It would be the first time I'd ever see my father descend into a dark depression.

SOMEONE SOMEWHERE WHO never had kids once came up with the misguided expression that "having a dog is just like having a kid."

It's not.

Over the years, I'd learned that my relationships with Nicholas and more recently Cleo could more or less be qualified as "simple." To me, that's meant to be more complimentary than condescending. With Cleo specifically, there is an elegance and effortlessness to her sense of companionship, and hence to our relationship, that's easy to summarize. It's steady and loyal and relatively unemotional. That's not to say that I don't love Cleo, but that my relationship with her lacks the mosaic of emotions that my other relationships— notably with humans—are made of.

My bond with Krishu is indescribable. While it's hard to put into words what exactly I feel for and with my son, *simple* certainly isn't the word. On those first days with him, when he'd sleep between

Candice and me, I'd find myself staring at him. Just staring. It started out as new parent vigilance. Wasn't it my job to ensure he was breathing and all systems were still go? But it evolved over time into a mix of objective fascination (look how he grows from day to day) to a total obsessive subjectivity. He was mine. I'd jokingly ask Candice if she really did love our son more every day like the old cliché predicted. She was steadfast, even in recent weeks when potty training had taken a turn for the worse, Krishu was all of a sudden pulling all-nighters, and his defiance had reached new heights.

Despite the jokes, I was miraculously the same way, to the point that I couldn't even fathom today how I could like the kid more tomorrow. Lo and behold though, when tomorrow came, the miracle just grew. To that extent, if my father's relationship with Daddy is to serve as a road map for mine with Krishu, then we were in for something very special. Papa's reverence for his father was unique. It was a combination of parental love and respect but also an admiration that transcended normal familial bonds.

"What was so special about Daddy?" I asked Papa over dim sum Sunday morning. It had been several years now since he'd died, but Daddy still regularly came up in conversation.

Papa thought about it for a beat. "He was wise. And he understood context."

It was a straightforward, albeit curious reply. I pressed Papa for more.

"There's a difference between intelligence and wisdom," Papa answered as he picked up some vegetables with his chopsticks. "Intelligence comes from having mastery over data and information. Wisdom comes from having mastery over intuition, emotion, time . . . and intelligence itself. It's about being plugged into the universe and knowing the right way to deal with the right circumstance at the right time. It manifests as a full understanding of the ecosystem in which one exists. Daddy always understood the context of a moment and how to react to it.

"That's why he was so wise."

When Daddy passed away, my whole family was devastated. He was the family patriarch, but in a very unassuming and gentle way. Even to those he was not connected to by blood, like my mother and her parents, Nani and Nana, the loss of Daddy was a crippling emotional blow. Not only was he the family doctor in every sense—he had overseen everyone's health, from every newborn to each of his own generation in the family as they aged—but also the gentleness, grace, patience, and yes, wisdom of his presence had affected everyone he'd ever touched.

When we were small Chota Papa once told us a story about Daddy that pretty much said it all. He recalled a time decades ago when he was about seven years old and Papa was ten and they lived in a rural part of India. As a military doctor, every few years Daddy was posted in different parts of India tending to soldiers and setting up medical units, often from scratch.

"Once a week," Papa recalled, when I asked him recently to tell me the story again, "on Sundays, Daddy would open up the clinic and allow entry to anyone who needed free medical assistance or advice.

"Over the years, he must have treated thousands of people that way. Some just had simple problems—cuts or wounds infected because of unhygienic care and conditions, while others had complex ailments that I've never seen to this day in all of my own medical experience."

It's no big leap to suggest that it was during this time, watching Daddy care gallantly for countless villagers, often changing their lives with the simple application of an antibiotic, a splint, or even some advice, that both Papa and Chota Papa determined their medical aspirations. To that end, Daddy's impact was profound and deep. While Papa would go on to get his acclaim, Chota Papa's achievements were not too shabby. He'd have his own illustrious career as a physician, culminating in his ongoing role as the dean of continuing education at Harvard Medical School. Yeah—*that* Harvard.

"And it wasn't just Daddy," Papa reminded me. "Ma was right by his side. Since so many people were coming to see Daddy from so far away, naturally there were long lines and people had to wait for hours. In order to make sure they didn't do so hungrily, Ma cooked huge amounts of food and then we—Chota Papa and me— served it while Ma listened to all of their problems. Together, we were quite the team."

Years later, Daddy received word that the army was posting him to another region.

"We packed up our things—we didn't have much, as we were used to living in places just temporarily—and headed for the train station. Chota Papa and I loved riding trains because Daddy would take us up onto the roof of the passenger cars so we could see the countryside as the train passed through it." I could tell from Papa's wistful nostalgia that these were among the most precious memories he had of days gone by.

"When we got to the train station, we were welcomed by the most amazing sight. Two thousand people had come to say goodbye. Most had brought food and sweets as gifts. The longer we waited for the train—Indian trains were notoriously delayed—the more people showed up until the whole platform was packed with well-wishers.

"When we finally got on the train and it pulled away, all of us—Ma, Daddy, Chota Papa, and me—waved out the windows to everyone. I still remember seeing dozens upon dozens of strangers weeping as the train left the station. That's how much Daddy had affected them."

Papa nodded with admiration. "I'll never forget that."

SOMEHOW OVER THE years I'd naively assumed that Papa could come up with an answer for every one of life's predicaments. Surely he knew how to manage the loss of a loved one. Hadn't he written a book about it somewhere along the way?

"I have, actually," Papa noted. "But knowing the rules doesn't make you a master of the game."

Indeed, when Daddy passed away—notably with no warning nor signs of ill health—papa was emotionally overwrought and propelled into a grief and philosophical questioning unlike he'd ever experienced. He admitted that it was the first time in his life he'd experienced insomnia. He'd spend long nights lying awake questioning the meaning of his life, his mortality, and whether he'd ever feel truly passionate about anything again.

He shrugged when I asked him about it. Even as I struggled to keep Krishu from tossing a dumpling that rolled around on his plate, I watched Papa. Very rarely in my life had I detected the sort of body language in him that I did at that moment. His shoulders slumped with indecision and his eyes lacked their usual conviction.

"I think it was something I just had to go through. Grief is a process. There's no other way to really deal with it."

Funny, I thought to myself when I later recalled Papa's response. I'd have expected something more profound, a self-generated (and no doubt Chopra-branded) truism or elegant quote from Rumi or Tagore. And yet the more I thought about it, the more I realized that the *process* itself that he cited was the true insight he'd stumbled upon. And once again Papa and Cleo had a lot in common, and dare I say, a certain wisdom about them when it came to dealing with the greatest human mystery there is: death.

AFTER CANDICE AND I got married, within a week after she graduated from medical school, we both packed up our respective New York apartments and moved across the country to Los Angeles with Cleo in tow. Having lived in a Beverly Hills apartment by myself for a few years, realizing quickly that it wasn't the right neighborhood for me, Candice and I sought a different neighborhood to start out our married life. Much to my surprise, actually, Papa had offered some sage advice.

"Make sure there are two sinks in the master bathroom," he offered soberly. "And, if possible, live near water or mountains," he added.

After an exhaustive search and considerably overshooting our budget, Candice and I found a rental that fit both of the criteria. With great trepidation we signed a year-long lease for a small one-bedroom apartment on a tiny Santa Monica street less than a block from the beach. In part we justified this expensive apartment selection by insisting that it would make Cleo much happier to live a leisurely beach life. A city dog her whole life, surely she should have sun and sand to soften the blow of being ripped away from her urban surroundings. The theory didn't follow any logic; still, it made writing the monthly rent check just a little easier.

Another attraction to the apartment was the neighborhood. It was actually on the second floor of a house on a street populated by other Craftsman homes, each one of which exuded a quaint flair and charm. The families ranged from an elderly couple who had lived on the street for almost forty years, to a young single actress I recognized (much to Candice's horror) from late-night Cinemax movies, to a couple in their late thirties who lived off an inheritance from her father. They spent their days homeschooling their two young sons and, in the process, became pseudo-ambassadors of our quiet street.

Candice and I learned these details from passive involvement with our neighbors, mostly awkward and inconvenient encounters when we were rushing from the house before or after work to walk Cleo. In retrospect, we were the quintessential frenzied New Yorkers living by the beach. Constantly rushing from one place to the next and usually late for something, we had laid down pretty much everything we had in our bank account to live by the beach, but we rarely, if ever, took the time to even put our toes in the sand. To us, our neighbors were akin to coinhabitants at the zoo. We might have been housed beside one another, but that didn't mean we had much in common aside from (possibly) being part of the same species.

Cleo, on the other hand, quickly assimilated herself to the new digs. Considering that she had spent her entire life up in the concrete jungle of New York City, this was somewhat surprising. Then again, Cleo's ability to integrate so easily to her surroundings was one of her more fascinating qualities. Whereas I had always understood dogs to be creatures of habit and routine—and Cleo was, in many respects—in this aspect she never really showed us any resistance or difficulty. Candice and I called her an "equal opportunity urinator," in that wherever we put the fancy Indian silk rugs that my mom had given us, Cleo peed on them. In doing so, she more than just marked her territory, she marked our home. That stale peanutty urine odor mixed with Nature's Miracle and Indian incense became the smell of familiarity for all of us. Aside from that, as long as Cleo had bowls to drink and eat from and a warm bed to sleep in (i.e., ours), her world would continue to spin on its axis.

In terms of how she interacted with others, neighbors included, Cleo operated in a relatively black-and-white world. Inside the house—her territory—anyone nonfamily was an open target for her terror. Being that she was so small and harmless, the object of her aggressions often didn't realize it, and quickly tamed Cleo with affection, which was her most overt kryptonite. Outside of the house, or I should say *outside*, Cleo was almost the exact opposite. She was exceedingly friendly, often pulling her leash toward others so that she could get sniffs and licks on any random pedestrian. This was largely the result of Cleo's discovery that during top dog-walking times—early mornings and early evenings—a lot of people in our hood carried doggy treats. Cleo knew just how to work these suckers.

First she'd approach her targets, cautiously sniffing around their feet or their dogs, her own tail wagging for all to see that she meant (good) business. If they showed any interest at all in her, she'd quickly turn on the charm and ratchet up her best *Gone with the Wind* affect, arching her neck upward, as if begging for affection. When she most often got it, she went for the kill, rolling over submissively and presenting her belly for a nice rubdown. By this time, she had her targets nailed. The tipping point was a mere formality: She'd roll back over, sit on her hind legs, and look upward with her giant precataract puppy dog eyes. If indeed the target had any treats, they were as good as gone.

Dogs, on the other hand, were of little interest to Cleo. Considering that most dogs didn't carry tote bags filled with their own treats, this wasn't all that surprising, I suppose. Sure, like all dogs, Cleo did the perfunctory routine when confronted with another dog—sniffing and inspecting, sometimes playing a little game of "twisting the leash" if the mood felt right—but by and large, her own species intrigued her hardly at all.

That's precisely why her relationship with the neighbor's dog Mocha (let alone basic acknowledgment of him) was so special. Mocha was an aptly named rescue dog that appeared to be some mixture of Labrador and, well, something else. He was at least twice the size of Cleo but apparently just as undisciplined, distinctive, and also harmless. His owner sheepishly confessed to me once that while Mocha had been neutered, it hadn't done much to settle him down. Sure, he wasn't horny, but that energy seemed only to have been channeled into an endless frenetic playfulness. If Cleo had a well thought out and deliberate Genghis Khan–esque routine to conquer all of Santa Monica and hoard its treats, Mocha was the exact opposite. He was a surfer dude, content with fun in the sun.

More remarkable, though, was the way in which Mocha interacted with Cleo. Because while his playfulness never left him— even when he chilled out with Cleo you could still see the twinkle in his eyes—with Cleo Mocha fell into line. Somehow, in some moment that I certainly hadn't witnessed, she had asserted herself as the alpha and Mocha took her lead.

Often when Cleo and I returned from walks, Mocha would be waiting outside of his house, tail wagging furiously as she came into sight. Initially this led us to allow the two of them to play in the same yard, jump around, rubbing snouts, chasing each other in circles, and sniffing each other in their downtime. Over time, as their relationship grew, we and our neighbors would leave the two of them together even when we were at work or out for the day. It was a new role for Cleo, to be the leader of the pack. She seemed to enjoy it. Wherever she walked, Mocha followed. Wherever she settled for a nice afternoon snooze, Mocha kept her in his sight line. She did the same. He was the only dog I'd ever seen Cleo actually allow to share her food and water bowls. These kids were made for each other.

All of this pleased Candice and me considerably. As part of our new married life, living in an apartment we couldn't really afford, we were both taking our professional lives very seriously. Entrenched already in her medical residency, Candice was rotating between multiple hospitals, which often meant late nights. Likewise, my hours were stretching at work, which translated into the two of us barely seeing each other at home after work before I'd have to hustle Cleo out of the house for her nightly walk. By the time I returned, Candice was usually already fast asleep.

The real casualty in all of this was Cleo. We both wanted to spend more time with her, but the realities of our new lives meant we couldn't. The fact that she had found a buddy in Mocha was a godsend to us all. Practically, it meant one less worry in our self-obsessed lives, knowing that Cleo seemed to be okay. And so, largely we figured we were off the hook when it came to worrying about her.

But then a strange thing happened. Cleo's mood changed. At first, as we had fallen into a pattern of comfort, it was hard to say where exactly it happened. But we detected little things. On the weekend—the time we did have with her and when we often liked to take long walks on the bike path along the beach—Cleo was lethargic and would constantly try to pull on the leash back toward the house. She was sleeping longer and more frequently. She ate next to nothing, uninterested even in the treats or Greenies that we offered her. When I attempted to instigate her to play, jumping in front of her or intoning my voice in the way she always reacted to, she just stared at me passively.

A week into this mystery, the revelation came to Candice. "Where's Mocha?"

We stared outside of our window into the neighbor's yard and saw no trace of him. We could even see into their house from ours and there too there was no sign of the crazy guy. It soon became clear that being the terrible neighbors that we were, we had failed to notice that Mocha was no more. When I sheepishly asked our neighbor what happened, he informed me with tears in his eyes that Mocha had passed away about ten days prior from a congenital defect. He died peacefully and painlessly overnight, our neighbor advised, kindly intimating that perhaps that was the reason we hadn't noticed.

I offered my condolences and retreated back to the house, where Candice sat with Cleo in her lap, stroking her gently. Not familiar with doggy depression, I immediately consulted the experts (the Internet) to see what I could find. Sure enough, Cleo had all the telltale signs.

Like humans, dogs mourn the loss of loved ones. In fact, in some ways, dogs can mourn even more intensely and certainly in more concentration than humans. Maybe it's because they do not bear the same burdens that we humans do. They don't have to worry about getting to work on time, returning home for dinner with the kids, maintaining a marriage, or paying the rent. They can immerse themselves in their emotion, let it seep straight through them. If you've ever been around a depressed dog—the way Cleo was after her buddy Mocha died—then you can physically see just how encompassing the emotions can be. Cleo sagged. Her ears, her tail, her eyes—anything that could play victim to gravity did. Her whole being drooped as if in solidarity with her mood.

Equally remarkable, however, was how Cleo emerged from her gloominess. A few days later—about two weeks in total after Mocha's death—Candice and I awoke to Cleo standing over us. The moment she saw my eyes open, her tail wagged furiously. I tried to turn over and go back to sleep, but it was too late. Cleo was a master of seizing *that* moment. Once she knew you were up, you were up. She leaped to the floor, scrambling to the side of the bed, growling at me anxiously.

"All right, Cleo, okay," I said, swinging my legs over the side of the bed. Now it was on—she knew where we were headed. For a walk. She barked excitedly, her tail in overdrive.

Candice sat up in bed staring down at her with a big smile.

"What?" I asked her, rubbing the sleep from my eyes.

"Nothing," Candice said, shaking her head. "Except that Cleo's back."

Sure enough, Cleo was back. Once more as we walked around the block, Cleo yanked and pulled me every few steps toward some curious item—a can or bottle, a french fry, a chewed-up piece of gum—so that she could inspect it as *the* most fascinating thing on planet Earth. When we encountered other early risers, Cleo was back in her fine form, alternatively begging for treats and tangling her leash with other dogs'.

I wondered what had happened. How had Cleo transitioned from her sad self back to her normal playful one? I watched closely as we neared the house, curious to see if there would be any acknowledgment of Mocha or his home. Sure enough, as we got to the gate, Cleo made a beeline to the fence that separated our house from Mocha's. She pressed her nose at the base of it. This was the spot where on the opposite side Mocha would do the same—the two of them exchanging a little signal or acknowledgment to the other one. This time, of course, there was no Mocha on the other side, but watching Cleo, you would have never known it. Her tailed wagged as she sniffed hard once or twice. Then suddenly, she jerked up and pulled away, leading me back into the house and on to our routine.

Back inside, life went on for us—Cleo, Candice, and me. Soon Candice and I were back at work, focused on what we had to get done, and Cleo likewise back to her antics and routine. Still, I liked to think that Mocha didn't just disappear from Cleo's consciousness, and her ritualized tribute of him every time we returned from our subsequent walks seemed to affirm that. But it did appear that in her own way Cleo had dealt with her grief over the loss of her friend, endured it, and in some ways resolved it so that she could move on.

Even in the death of a friend, Cleo appeared to have brought that same clarity of emotion. Her engagement with the world and all of her emotions tied into it came with an ease and effortlessness that was truly admirable. In honoring death, she'd found new life and we had our lovable, feisty, and crazy Cleo back.

IT'S RARE, IF EVER, that death is expected. Even in cases when it arrives with some warning, a doctor's diagnosis or some odd premonition, death almost always requires a denouement and reflection. After returning from brunch, I brewed a pot of coffee while Papa and I sat in the backyard watching Cleo and Krishu skip around the small plastic playhouse we had recently constructed. The two of them could spend hours in such activity, Krishu chasing Cleo in circles while she wagged her tail, always maintaining a safe enough distance so that she wouldn't risk actually being caught by him. As he was still not fully in control of his own body, Cleo was wise enough to ensure that she never literally fell into his clutches. But this time, as they went around the far corner of the elevated rock platform where our gardeners had just planted some new fruit trees, Cleo suddenly stopped. Something in the bushes had distracted her. She skipped off the path, poking her head into leaves, and suddenly the tone of her bark changed. I knew something was wrong. I leaped from my chair, rushing over to where the two of them stood. Pulling Krishu back and picking him up, I peered toward where Cleo had been rustling.

"What is it, Cleo?"

As she backed away, I could finally see it. The body of a dead bird lay on the ground, just slightly concealed by some leaves. The moment I seemed to see and acknowledge it, Krishu did too.

Papa lingered behind us. "What?"

I pointed to the bird and Papa surveyed it.

"Oh."

We stood there for a quiet beat. It was Krishu who broke the silence. "Papa—what happened?"

What happened was among the first noun-verb constructions Krishu had managed to pull off.

"If you think about it, it's the quintessential question to all of existence," Papa would later remark. "The cosmos is an exquisite ribbon of synchronistic happenings. *It* happened."

This was likely Krishu's first brush with death. Only in *Kung Fu Panda* had he encountered the notion, but when Master Oogway kicked it, he did it with considerable pomp and pageantry, his body quickly disappearing in a swirl of shimmering golden rose petals. No one needed to question what happened next.

I pulled Krishu back, ordered Cleo away as well. Papa, however, loitered, staring at the lifeless bird as if with a fascination that moved him.

"Let him see it," Papa called back to me. " 'Death is an undiscovered country from whose bourn no traveler returns.' "

"That's creepy," I said.

"That's Shakespeare," he replied.

"Papa, he's two."

"Death stalks us all. Never too early to encounter it."

Krishu stared at the carcass, confused. Death was literally not part of his vocabulary, neither in language nor conception, really. I could see the wheels turning as he tried to process what he was witness to. At last I swept him from his feet and took him inside.

Later that evening, sometime after I had convinced my father that it was rather macabre to quote Shakespeare on death to his two-year-old grandson, Papa and I sat in the living room watching the news.

Cleo lay on my lap, her eyes blankly fixed on the flashing lights of the television. I always wondered what exactly shot through her brain as she consumed the sights and sounds of the television. Presumably she was neither a fan of Anderson Cooper nor a critic of Bill O'Reilly the way I was. And yet, she gazed at the TV with a fixed stare that rivaled the very best poker players. Whether she was emotionally swayed—saddened or enraged—by news of another suicide bombing on the streets of Kabul was anyone's guess.

"Cleo is not victim to the hallucination of social conditioning. She is not held hostage by the same rules and rituals that signify how we should celebrate life or commemorate death."

"You mean she's not fooled by the Matrix?" I nodded back to him.

"What?" Papa looked at me confused.

"Nothing." I shook my head.

He continued undeterred. "One of Cleo's greatest attributes is precisely her 'dogginess.' She's not burdened by the angst of being human, the self-doubt, the ambition, the guilt, the nagging feeling that there is a greater dharma to her existence or her demise.

"Even with death, she does not evaluate. She reacts."

I told Papa about Cleo and Mocha, the seeming depression that she endured in the aftermath of her friend's death, and how she seemed, suddenly, to snap out of it.

"Mourning is a process." Papa tapped his fingers on the couch. "Its various stages include denial, anger, frustration, resignation, acceptance, surrender—and hopefully, if all of the above have been resolved—healing.

"Most people get so distracted by their lives and all their obligations that they are not able to make it through the process. And hence they never fully recover from the loss of a loved one. They become emotionally frayed, strands of unresolved grief and loss that linger and line their daily existence."

The silence sat between us.

"I think what's unique about Cleo is that she's fully in touch with her feelings, not distracted by all the other obligations that we are. When Mocha left her, she took the time to endure the process, to navigate the stages of her own emotions and arrive at her own healing. There's a wisdom in that." Papa nodded.

"Knowing the right way to deal with the right circumstance at the right time," I offered.

Papa smiled. "Exactly."

"Part of our discomfort with death is that it is a reminder to all of us of the impermanence of our own lives. For most people, their own mortality is their greatest fear and the death of a loved one is also the death of a small part of the self.

"Cleo—dogs in general—are intensely loyal to their owners. But they also have a great sense of self. They recognize the boundary between themselves and others, even at an emotional level if not a fully conscious and intellectual one. It's actually a beautiful thing, because it allows them to be bonded with people, highly intuitive of the emotional climate around them, but also in touch with their own senses. It's quite fantastic, actually—something to aspire to."

"What about you, Papa?" I interrupted him as he marveled at

Cleo's emotional intelligence once more. "Are you healed from Daddy's death?"

Papa paused, thinking to himself. Death is indeed complicated. He exhaled heavily, a swell of emotion forming in his eyes. "I'm doing the best that I can."

eight

What's the one thing I should teach Krishu?

The one and only thing that is truly important is that he should be himself. Being in touch with one's self and comfortable with who you are enables a person to radiate simple unaffected humanity. There is nothing more lovable or more charming or more evolutionary than not having to put on a social mask. That simple unaffected humanity or comfort with your own identity allows a person to behave spontaneously and effortlessly and meet the challenges of life with joyfulness, courage, and confidence no matter what comes their way.

IT HAD BEEN A WHILE SINCE WE'D HEARD FROM MY mother. Considering that pretty much all of my life we'd spoken several times a day, I was oddly comforted by the silence. To me it meant that there was nothing significant for her to report, that Nana's recovery must have been on track. That all changed when I got a call from my father.

"Have you spoken to your mother?"

"No," I replied. "Not for a few days. Why?"

Pause.

"I can't reach her."

He sounded uneasy. I knew this tone well, especially as it related to my father being able to reach my mother. For a man who spent so much time traveling by himself to far-off places, it was a curious irony. Papa liked to know my mother's whereabouts and grew paranoid when he went more than two hours without speaking to her, even when he didn't have anything in particular to say.

Yes, *two hours,* the duration of your average movie. This very issue has been a significant one in my parents' marriage. My mother loves to see movies and my father hates not being able to speak to her whenever he wants to. And yet, despite this overwhelming challenge, they persevere.

"I'm sure everything's fine," I reassured Papa. "I mean . . . if it wasn't, then she would have called."

"Yeah," he agreed. "You're right."

But as I hung up the phone, I was the uneasy one. I tried my mom on her cell but predictably it went unanswered. I went to sleep that night with a bad feeling in the pit of my stomach. Sure enough, about an hour later, just after midnight, the phone rang. It was my mother.

"Is everything okay?" I asked, before she could even really say anything.

"Nana's back in the hospital," she answered.

I didn't know how to respond.

"He wasn't feeling well, couldn't get out of bed, and became disoriented. It may just be dehydration, but . . ." Her voice trailed off.

"But what!?" I wanted to blurt out, but didn't, sensing my mom didn't want to say anything further.

"They're doing some tests," she said. "I wanted to know what we're dealing with before I called, but it may take a few days."

She was stressed. She was unsure what she was dealing with and it had formed a thick fog of angst around her.

I wanted to say something reassuring, but couldn't find the words.

We chatted for a few minutes, me sharing stories about the milestones Krishu had passed, Mom updating me on our relatives in India. But I could tell she was weary. It wasn't just the ambiguity of Nana's health. It was being away from home, from her grandkids, who had become her lifeline in recent years. From Papa too. She asked how he was doing.

"Good." I nodded as I said it, as if she could see me from the other side of the planet. There wasn't much point to saying anything more. She could be half a world away, as she was, and still know exactly how Papa was doing.

Mom said she'd call as soon as she had any news on Nana's condition. She told me to give a big kiss to Krishu, and then she said good night. I rolled back over and gave my sleeping boy that kiss right then and there. But I couldn't sleep. In fact, I tossed and turned all night, which would prove to be a very bad thing, considering what was waiting for me.

MORNING LOG 8/1/09

Dog wakes up at 4:46 a.m.
Baby wakes up at 4:47 a.m.
Baby pees on bedroom floor.
Dog shits on playroom floor.
Baby pees on bathroom floor.

Baby and dog fight over sausage.

Dog wins.

Baby cries.

Papa (Deepak) wakes up and decides to walk to Starbucks.

Baby pees on living room floor.

Dog sleeps.

Baby wants Mama.

Papa (Gotham) exhausted.

AS THE FATHER of an infant, I had discovered that Monday mornings had become the new Friday nights. No longer was there any other part of the week that I looked forward to more than Monday at nine a.m., when our wonderful nanny arrived to take Krishu off our hands. After weekends spent in the never-ending routine of entertaining the boy, cleaning up after the boy, and cleaning up the boy, I anticipated the Monday morning reprieve like an eleventh-hour phone call from the governor.

I was not alone in this. On Monday mornings I'd detect in Candice a distinctive spring in her step, a renewed energy to get out the door and to the office as soon as she possibly could. Which explains why, when the perfect storm hit us that August morning, no amount of lollipops (Krishu's kryptonite) could stave off my own personal Lex Luthorian doomsday. The prior night, our nanny had called to say she wasn't feeling well and was unlikely to be able to come to work. Being that it was the infamous summer of H1N1, we urged her to stay away. Candice, meanwhile, was summoned to the hospital at four in the morning to consult on a patient who had been involved in a car accident. That left me to manage Monday morning on my own. Cue the apocalypse.

I had always rationalized that I'd pick up this "parenting thing" when, you know, I became a parent. The way I looked at it, so far so good. Both Cleo and Krishu were alive and seemingly well. If nothing else, I took great pride in this approach because it contrasted so starkly with my wife's more regimented philosophy. In other words, I got to be the good guy, a role I thought I played pretty well and which gave me great self-esteem, even if it made my wife occasionally hate me. The downside was that she got to revel in moments when she knew her strict approach wasn't available to counterbalance my more laissez-faire technique. She knew better than anyone that, left on our own, especially at key times when both Krishu and Cleo craved her rituals and a consistent routine, a mother of a meltdown would occur. And I'd have to take my medicine.

Meanwhile, Papa's presence over the past weeks had added a new energy to the mix. Cleo, in particular, regarded him with a mixture of warmth and suspicion. On the one hand, Papa was another person to bully for treats, to take her for walks, and to study like the seasoned anthropologist she had become. Because Papa wasn't necessarily wise to her ways, she could manipulate him, thereby exploiting this weakness in the household.

But there was a downside for the pup. Papa might have been a soft touch for treats, but he wasn't fully up on her rituals and routines. For instance, when Cleo would snuggle up to Papa, as she was wont to do with any warm body, he generally moved away in short order. She reacted to this with a combination of confusion and irritation. Why wouldn't he want her odor pasted to his? And why was he denying her his body heat?

Cleo got the message all right. She'd retreat elsewhere and do whatever it is she did when Papa slighted her, but inevitably she'd come back and try again. No shame. No hard feelings. If at first you don't succeed . . .

These routines weren't confined to Cleo and Papa. They were a pervasive part of all the relationships in the house, notably Krishu and Cleo's. As Krishu mowed through countless milestones of physical, cognitive, and emotional development—feeling out his boundaries, learning to express himself through language, managing his own coordination—Cleo evolved her behavior around his. It wasn't just about staying alert, maintaining physical space, or planning quick getaways, it was about calibrating her own emotions and reactions toward him.

Our weekends had become a ceaseless therapy session that involved negotiating feuds between Cleo and Krishu, separating them, reprimanding them, reuniting them—rinse, lather, repeat. The most fascinating aspect of this merry-go-round was that neither Cleo nor Krishu ever seemed to tire of it. No matter how heated things became, no matter how many tears, snarls, fists, or snaps, after a few minutes of downtime, they'd reposition their chin straps and dig their heels in once more.

When Papa finally returned from his Starbucks expedition—he had wisely disappeared for over an hour—he witnessed firsthand another common interaction between Krishu and Cleo. As Krishu ate his breakfast—waffles soaked in syrup—Cleo stood devotedly by his feet hoping he would toss her a few scraps. Krishu's concentration, however, was fixed on the TV screen, where my mistress in times like these (also known as Dora the Explorer) cheerfully distracted him for thirty minutes at a time. Singularly focused, Krishu showed little likelihood of sending anything Cleo's way. Cleo knew this, and slid behind him to see if she might snake a syrupy square away from his plate. On second thought, remove the doubt. By hook or by crook, Cleo was going to get her waffle on.

Watching Cleo, it was obvious why the term is "cat burglar" and not "dog burglar." She had no vanity about her technique, no desire for style. In that sense she was spartan. For Cleo it was about getting the job done, about bringing home the goods. Hind legs firmly planted for a solid foundation, front legs nimbly perched onto Krishu's miniature table, she positioned herself straight for her main target, while maintaining enough balance to maneuver out of his crosshairs should he catch on.

He caught on.

Timing, as they say, is everything. With Krishu between bites and Dora apparently taking a beat herself, Krishu reached back for another waffle square but got instead a fluffy-headed, wet-nosed waffle thief.

"Let go of my Eggo," his eyes screamed.

Simple defiance in Cleo's.

Outrage.

One of Krishu's recent milestones, despite our repeated reminders that we "shared everything" in our home, was a strong sense of possessiveness. In recent weeks, "Mine!" had become a constant exclamation around the house. It wasn't just waffles. It was toys, clothes, furniture, even people. Notably his Oedipus complex had kicked in, for Candice had ceased to exist in any context outside of Krishu. Any mention of her as "my wife" antagonized him to no end. He'd hear nothing of it. She was *his* mama, *his* wife, *his* aunt, *his* daughter, *his* friend, or whatever other qualifier we could possibly come up with.

Back to the waffle: Cleo's snatch and grab had been compromised. She was caught red-handed, trying to pilfer *his* waffles. She had no defense. In matters like these, Krishu was Taliban-like. Punishment was stiff, harsh, and swift. In this instance, she also had no wiggle room—not just metaphorically, but literally. Lured and distracted by Aunt Jemima's forbidden fruit, Cleo had not thought out her fail-safe option. She had no escape plan. By sneaking behind Krishu, she had confined herself between the wall, the couch, the table, and him. She was cornered.

"My waffle!" he shouted, reaching for the square that hung from Cleo's mouth.

Flashing her agility, she dodged him. It was an impressive stall, but just a temporary one. Because still, she had nowhere to go: Krishu had her wedged in and he knew it.

He reached for the waffle again, this time even more forcefully. Still not the master of his own anatomy, he missed the sugary treat and landed his open palm on Cleo's snout. Candice and I had become more attentive in detecting Krishu's recent aggression with Cleo, doing our best to defuse the situation and/or break up brewing trouble whenever we could. But every so often the laws of the jungle took over and physical violence gripped our household. It wasn't pretty, nor something we were proud of. But then again, we told ourselves, life on the streets of Santa Monica was not always easy. Survival of the fittest and all that.

Krishu and Cleo went at it, but in the end it was Cleo's raw survival skills that won out. Every dog has her day, and on this day the dog had her waffle too. In the aftermath of the epic struggle, Cleo limped away with a soft but triumphant whimper while Krishu erupted in a monsoon of devastation and shame.

Papa, witness to this dramatic unfolding, was at a loss for words. But not for long.

"It's *Leela*," he announced, describing the relationship between Krishu and Cleo. Leela is the name of Krishu's older sister, Mallika's daughter, but in this case it was the deeper meaning of the word that papa was invoking. *Leela* means "the play of the universe."

"More specifically," Papa said with a nod, "it means the exquisite dance of all creation, the cosmos inhaling and exhaling, the interaction of everything and everyone in the universe."

"How so?" I asked as I consoled Krishu by promising to make him some turkey sausages.

"Because . . ." Papa pointed toward Cleo, who had wolfed down whatever waffle she had managed to get away with. Her tail wagged with renewed energy as she slowly returned ready to play with Krishu one more time.

"Cleo—like the universe—doesn't hold grudges. She knows how to forgive and evolve."

WHILE IT'S HARD to recall what life was like before the ceaseless storm of parenting, there once was a time when Candice and I lived a more adventurous life. Several years into our marriage, after she at long last completed her medical training in Los Angeles, we decided to move to India for a few months. It wasn't an easy decision, but the timing felt right. Candice had just completed almost a decade's worth of schooling and the next inevitable step was to get a job and start working. We both knew that once she started that path, it would be hard to get off it. Meanwhile, I had launched a new and exciting media company with two friends. The company was primarily based in India, which, while I had visited almost every year since I was alive, I had never really spent considerable time in as an adult. To me, India was where my parents were from, where my grandparents lived, and where my ancestors had toiled. It wasn't particularly a place where I felt at home, and yet so much of the culture and thinking that anchored my life had its roots there. If there ever was a time to really experience India more intimately, this was it. There was only one problem. Cleo.

Cleo had become our fixture and companion. She was our third wheel and our best friend. Still, despite the depth of our feelings for her, Candice and I both knew it was now or never with India. It certainly wasn't our intention to move there for good, but we also didn't want to have a rigid time line for our return. India had been a land of obligation until that point. Most of our visits had been for the purposes of attending family weddings, weeklong affairs that involved party after party, ritual after ritual, and made doing anything else—especially traveling away from New Delhi, where my family was based—just plain impossible.

This time, however, Candice was excited by the prospects of traveling to different parts of the country, going on adventurous pilgrimages to sacred sites, more rural regions, and various other exotic locales in the mountains of the north, the deserts of the east, and the seaside cities of the south. Meanwhile, I wanted not just the freedom to focus on work and the new company, but to really connect with India's soul. To me, India was not just the land of my ancestors, but increasingly as the years passed I realized that its lore, culture, and traditions were a dynamic part of my own being. There were parts of my own self that I was discovering just by familiarizing myself with the stories and culture of India. I was hungry for more. It was an itch and I wanted to scratch it.

Before we left for our trip, Candice and I flew to Atlanta to deliver Cleo to Candice's mother, who lived there. Their reunion was another example of Cleo's curious recognition of family. Even though she only saw Candice's mother intermittently, maybe once every six months on average, she was emotionally bonded to her in a way that defied explanation—or at least my amateur ability to do so. In this instance, there was no period of reacquaintance or familiarization between them. Cleo's immediate exuberance upon seeing Candice's mother rivaled only what she exhibited when she was reunited with Candice after they'd been separated. Her tail wagged furiously and she elicited rapid high-pitched yelps as if she could not properly express her excitement. Finally, as was her custom though we had tried to train her not to, she hopped on her hind legs, grasping at my mother-in-law, struggling to land as many licks and kisses as possible. It was precisely the reason why we had determined that the only possible person Cleo could stay with while we were away was Candice's mom. The perks and comforts in her life in Atlanta would be plenty. Together they'd go on long walks a few times a day. They'd eat at outdoor cafes and frolic in dog parks. And at night, Cleo would not be remanded to some dog quarters or elaborate dog bed that she didn't care for; she could expect a place on the master bed itself, just the way it was at home. In fact, we rationalized, Cleo was probably better off this way. Candice and I had been so wrapped up in our lives recently and we hadn't been spending the time we once had with Cleo. Her walks were no longer neighborhood excursions, but rather quick bombing runs where she was expected to drop her payload within half a block, after which we'd hustle home. In Atlanta, Cleo was going to get so much undivided attention from Candice's mom, who was freshly retired and was still trying to figure out how to fill her days. We were killing two birds with one stone. Each of them would be happier to have the other.

At least that's what we told ourselves.

Not surprisingly, Candice articulated this better than I, wondering aloud at the last minute if we should pull the plug on the whole thing. That our excitement for our big adventure was tangled with so much emotional baggage and guilt was a constant sore spot for both of us. We both claimed to love Cleo so much. And yet, there we were so easily leaving her for however long our wanderlust would fuel us in exotic India. Would we ever do such a thing with our child? both of us wondered separately. Definitely not. Yet again, there we were shamefully excited about our upcoming Indian adventure.

While these mixed emotions flowed like the ocean tide in me, back and forth, back and forth, some deeper sense convinced me that it was indeed the right move for us at the right time.

"Yes, Candice," I declared with false bravado. "We *have* to go. And we *have* to leave Cleo. She'll be fine."

Several days later when we at last boarded our flight for India and crammed ourselves into our cramped seats, Candice turned to me and asked, "Do you think Cleo's angry at us?"

For days, I had wondered the same thing. We both were surprised when during our parting with her in Atlanta, Cleo had been cold and distant. When I had picked up Cleo to kiss her good-bye, I hadn't even earned a lick in return. It was enormously unlike her.

Sensing though that Candice remained deeply conflicted about our journey, I insisted that she was imagining things. In fact, Candice's mother had assured us that Cleo was fine. She'd adjusted well to the house and even forced Candice's father out of the master bed and into the basement, a sure sign that she was asserting herself with confidence and comfort. Sure, our parting had been tinged with awkwardness, but rage toward the family was not really part of her emotional arsenal.

Thinking back, the only time in Cleo's life I had actually witnessed her express serious anger or malice toward anyone was years prior, when Candice was in medical school. Enraged at Candice's roommate's dog, Sampson, who was from the same litter and constantly bothered her and ate from her food bowl, Cleo in front of all who were watching proceeded to his bed, squatted, and pissed in it. Then after Candice punished her and washed the dog bed, Cleo did it again.

On the surface it was an act of defiance and rage that was a bit unnerving. But I actually found myself quietly impressed by her willfulness. Sampson had clearly crossed some Rubicon with her and she was letting him know she wasn't just going to roll over. For a dog who, well, so easily rolled over, to know that she had some sacred boundaries was reassuring. I concluded at the time that Cleo was more than capable of understanding certain events and acting on those emotions if she felt so moved.

In this instance, though, I just couldn't convince myself that Cleo had it in her to direct that same anger toward us, let alone harvest a grudge while we were away. While I had the utmost respect for my dog, that sort of emotional vindictiveness and cerebral complexity certainly seemed beyond her.

I reassured Candice that Cleo would be just fine with her mother and that we really should've been excited about the journey in front of us. We had determined that we would base ourselves out of Bangalore, a bustling city in the south of India where my company's operations were based. Being of northern stock, I'd really never visited much of the southern portion of the country, which by reputation had very much its own distinct culture and feel. Candice too had already planned a number of excursions, some of which I would join her on, and others she intended on embarking with various friends and family members. With all of this in the works, and for us to fully embrace it, I sensed we needed a clean emotional slate, to not be weighed down by guilt or second thoughts. For Candice especially, I wanted her to be fully free of the rigid constraints of the prior decade, when her life had been regulated by the rigors and deadlines of the academic and medical world.

To that extent, everything went perfectly. Candice and I spent just about six months in India. I managed to stay relatively focused on the company, interacting and networking throughout Bangalore and Bombay in a way that I had never before. Candice sprinkled the months with excursions to a long list of temples, tea plantations, a jungle safari, a pilgrimage site, and even a stint observing doctors and volunteering at a famed medical clinic run by some missionaries. All in all, we got what we paid for. More than just immersing myself in Start-up 101 or Candice getting away from textbooks and emergency rooms, we both had needed our own detoxification. Back in LA, life had become consumed by stress. Our energy had become so cluttered—so many motives—that it was difficult to understand why we did anything anymore.

Papa had once told me that most people in life ended up "working hard at a job they don't really enjoy to buy stuff they don't really need to impress people they don't really like." I had seen myself doing just that before India allowed me to reflect on what it was that really mattered to me.

Over the course of the six months we were away, we'd check in with Candice's mom every few days. We'd ask how she was enjoying her new life post-retirement, what activities she had gotten herself involved in, and news surrounding the rest of the family. Really, though, what was most important to us was finding out how Cleo was doing. Without exception, the reports were the same. Cleo was happy as a clam.

It was toward the end of our fifth month in India that Candice and I took a road trip from Bangalore to a village famed for the Nadi astrologers who dwelled there. The Nadi are one of the countless phenomena that lurk all over India, a land where science and spirituality coexist unlike in any other part of the world. Today a city like Bangalore nurtures and generates some of the sharpest minds in the world, masters of physics, computer engineering, and technology, and exports them to the top companies in the world. At the same time, it seems that all of these kids—and most of them are indeed kids—live by spiritual and religious codes that defy the very science and theories that define the rest of their lives. They themselves don't see any contradiction between the two. If anything they are complementary: The same underlying intelligence that orchestrates the universe also animates its deeper mysteries.

The Nadi, a sect of astrologers descended from an ancient lineage, claim the ability to read the fortunes of all the visitors who come to them. The fortunes themselves are scrawled on old palm leaves rolled up into scrolls and archived in seven different locations around India, one of which Candice and I were visiting.

Here's how it works: Each visitor provides nothing more than a fingerprint, the right one for men and the left one for women. No names, no Social Security numbers, PINs, passwords, or other locator numbers. Based on those fingerprints, the Nadi astrologers recover a corresponding scroll (to each individual) and proceed to read from it the "story of your life."

Unbelievable?

You bet, and precisely the reason Candice and I decided it was a trip we had to make. With such spectacular mystery surrounding the Nadi, not to mention the majestic lore from which it stemmed, I had expected a most glorious setting for our prophetic readings. But once again India proved most contradictory. Rather than an elaborate mystical abode, after several hours' drive Candice and I found ourselves in a dusty little village of decrepit storefronts separated by narrow dirt roads. The legendary Nadi readers themselves, whom I had mentally fashioned as sage-like mystics with wizened beards and dressed in flowing saffron robes, were, in fact, instead sleepy Sadhus who chain-smoked native bidi cigarettes and chirped on cell phones when not on the clock. We had brought with us a young Indian translator named Mishra. He was native to the region, spoke the language, and knew the roads. He was eager to please and knowledgeable about the history and culture of that part of India. Noting my blank expression, he smiled. "Just like your Disneyland, no?"

After being offered flat sodas and sickly sweet Indian desserts, Candice and I were escorted into a dilapidated structure where droning chants from a portable CD player echoed off the yellow walls. Before formally starting, Mishra confided that the readings were generally done in private, involving only the reader, the visitor, and the translator.

"You just never know what's on the scroll." He spoke with a tone that suggested informed experience. "It's not just the skeletons from the past that may lurk in your closet, but possibly future ones as well."

I wasn't sure how to react to this. Candice and I were pretty open with each other. Neither of us had significant secrets buried in our pasts (at least as far as I knew). However, the thought of future secrets being revealed was quite the mind twister. As it turns out, that was just the tip of the iceberg. Though in this case, the iceberg actually sat in a sticky south Indian village.

Those who have studied the Nadi, Papa included, explain the phenomena with a mixture of mystical terminology and quantum physics. "Inside every individual, the genetic memory of the whole cosmos is contained. There's a broader architecture to the universe and everything in it that connects all living things."

Consciousness, if you're keeping score at home.

"When you extract a little piece of information from an individual, it's like a holographic representation of the whole organism. If you know how to read it—and the Nadis do—then conceivably it makes perfect sense that they should be able to see the course that any individual life will take."

Perfect sense, right? There is, of course, so much to try and understand about the nature and mechanics of astrology, a system of prophecy, soothsaying, and science that has fascinated human civilization almost since its conception. Is it so far-fetched to suggest that we are indeed stitched into the fabric of the universe, that there is an intrinsic connection between the individual and the cosmos? This is the basic premise that the science of astrology assumes. Add some ritual, a few chants here and there, a ceremony that involves some formality, and you end up with something like the Nadis. The mystique and mythology that surrounds them is at once invigorating and also intimidating. That's why, when Mishra advised us to do it a certain way, we were inclined to take him at his word.

A young English-speaking woman appeared and offered her translating services to Candice for a modest price, leaving me with Mishra and his ubiquitous toothy smile.

Over the course of the next hour or so, Candice and I sat through our respective readings. The experience was nothing short of jaw-dropping. For both of us, our scrolls were uncannily accurate. Each of us had our birthdates and the circumstances surrounding them (locations, parents' names, exact timings) correctly identified. The fact that Candice's parents both had decidedly non-Indian names—Josephine and Hyland—and they were correctly (phonetically) identified on the scroll was astonishing. For me, obscure details from my adolescence, including the litany of sports-related injuries—broken fingers, twisted ankles, torn rotator cuff, ripped ligaments—were literally spelled out on my scroll.

Indeed our Nadi experience did anything but disappoint. For all those who had described it to us as the most amazing thing they'd ever experienced, our few hours with them certainly met those lofty standards and more. Along with the game-show-like revelations from our pasts that hit the bull's-eye, there were also prophetic-like predictions of the future, including work-related ups and downs, children, and yes, even death. Indeed it would take a book by itself to delve into the details surrounding the readings, not to mention the mythology and mechanics that surround them (including, of course, the many critics who dismiss the Nadis as nothing more than ancient hucksters).

Among the most incredulous portions of the readings occurred when the astrologer read from a specific section of the scroll that supposedly corresponded with my "past life." As the theory goes, these individual identities that we take on in the course of a singular life are nothing more than roles that we temporarily play. It struts and frets its hour upon the stage, but then fades into a far greater context. The real self is the role player beneath and it is timeless and immortal. Hindu theology proposes—and Nadi astrology certainly subscribes to Hindu doctrine—that an individual soul will spend numerous lives via reincarnation in pursuit of higher learning. Ultimately the goal is to arrive at a point where this cycle of reincarnation is no longer necessary, where true wisdom has been achieved, and the individual soul folds back into the collective one. The CliffsNotes version is that you want to be closer to the end than the beginning.

It was with this context that midway during my reading, my astrologer announced that I was a relatively evolved soul.

"Relative to what?" I asked.

"No questions," the reader blurted, irritated. For the most part, the Nadi asrologers don't take questions. They read what's on the scrolls, nothing more. They don't claim to be architects of the universe, just that they have the skill to read the blueprints. My reader proceeded to rattle on in Tamil, the south Indian dialect that I couldn't understand in the least.

After a beat, my translator turned to me. "He says that you are doing a good job in this life. Coming closer to *moksha*—spiritual liberation." Mishra nodded his approval. "Good job."

"Thank you." I smiled. I wasn't sure what else to say. Who didn't like to have their spiritual parking ticket validated, if even they weren't sure what it all meant?

"He says"—Mishra swiveled his head in the way only Indians can, somewhere in between a nod and a shake—"to make sure you listen closely to your god."

Okay. I nodded, confirming my piety. My god? I wondered to myself. I'm not very religious. If you asked me 100 times which god I was going to lay this one on, you likely would have gotten 100 different answers. The 162-game baseball season had confirmed this, in fact, for the amount of times I had cut deals with gods, swearing never to ask again, was well into triple digits.

"Which God?"

Again the astrologer didn't wait for Mishra.

"D-O-G." He looked at me with his brow furrowed.

I stared back at him confused. "Dog?"

"G-O-D," he spat back, even more annoyed.

"Okay." I nodded. "But you said D-O-G just then," I pointed out. I looked at Mishra for confirmation. He gaped blankly back.

"Yes." The astrologer nodded vigorously. "Dog. D-O-G." He stared at me.

I'd always been terrible at staring contests growing up. Mallika regularly stared me down whenever we played. I had no chance against this guy. It was as if he were channeling the gods themselves. And he seemed angry.

Still I remained confounded. I knew what I had heard. I turned back to Mishra. "I think he said *God* but then he spelled *Dog*, right?"

"Maybe your dog is your god?" He smiled at me.

"Not *my* dog." I laughed. "She's not even trained to roll over." Mishra looked blankly back at me. We might as well have been speaking about obscure baseball statistics like on-base or slugging percentages: He neither understood what I was talking about, nor did he care. In his world, I was just another interloper into the Disney World of Indian mysticism.

But I had a feeling. I shook my head. "Mishra—can you just ask him? Did he mean *dog* or *god*?"

Mishra shrugged his shoulders and turned back to the astrologer. But before he could even ask, the astrologer interrupted him harshly.

"No questions!"

The *dog-god* anagram may as well have been the highlight of my Nadi reading. There were other details about my future that ensued, but I perhaps purposely didn't hear them or never let them imprint too much on my consciousness. I preferred the free will approach to life. Reunited in the car ride back, Candice and I compared notes. Predictably, some things aligned, while others confused us even more.

"Did Cleo come up at all in your reading?" I asked Candice hesitantly.

She laughed. "Sort of."

"What do you mean?"

"The guy said I was kindred spirits with Cleopatra. Either you should watch your back or he was talking about Cleo." She shrugged, unconcerned by this troubling disparity.

My mind too, however, had moved on.

"I think it's time to go home."

"We are going home." Candice nodded.

"No, I mean back to America. Back to Cleo."

. . .

A FEW DAYS LATER, packed into our tiny seats on our flight to the United States, Candice turned to me.

"You know when you said we should go home, you equated Cleo with it? That's really sweet. Does that mean Cleo and I are now your family? Your home?"

I was boxed in. I mustered all that I could to ensure that I didn't respond with some greeting card platitude like "Home is where the heart is . . ."

But she was right and we both knew it. Practically speaking, there wasn't much that we were going back to. No house, no jobs, no community of friends who had been missing us all of these months. Our parents and siblings were all relatively cosmopolitan globe-trotters themselves. They would hardly be waiting for us at the airport with banners and fruitcakes.

I once asked my father to define the concept of home. If you didn't have a big mortgage or lived a lifestyle that was not so anchored to a single neighborhood and community like we did, then the traditional definition felt unaligned.

"Home is a state of consciousness," he said. "It's what emotionally anchors us, where we feel most at ease. It's the people or places in whose reflection we see, or aspire to see, our own best qualities."

The more I thought about it on that flight back from India, the more the shoe fit. Over the near decade that we had had her, Cleo had become a part of my emotional balance. She had gone from being the dog I had had serious doubts about in the first place to becoming a central part of the life Candice and I envisioned building together. Indeed, she embodied so many of the qualities—

loyalty, trust, bliss, presence, and more—that I admired and aspired toward.

I knew at that moment that the act of going back to America, back to Cleo, was an admission of a new life stage. While the notion of "settling down" remains foreign to me even today, there was no doubt on that flight that I was headed toward a new and significant "grown-up phase" of our lives. Candice and I had both talked about starting a family and the Nadis had confirmed it was imminent. Candice was also likely to start a new job. And my company had moved from start-up to survival stage. All of the above would require a significantly new amount of focus and energy. I was actually excited about it. The grand design of the universe was indeed convening around us.

But there might be a hitch.

Candice ripped me from my gleeful optimism. "What if Cleo is really pissed off at us for leaving her?"

We gave it some thought.

"I mean, it's been six months . . ."

For the remainder of the flight, the thought lingered. In my brave new world where Cleo was synonymous with the concept of home, where she was declared my god by the Fates (literally), I had failed to account for the notion that she might be one angry and vindictive bitch.

IF CLEO DID have any resentment toward Candice and me, she stored it very well, presumably scheming to unleash it on us at a more strategic moment (we're still waiting). In fact, quite the contrary ensued. This time, Candice's mom brought her back to us in Los Angeles and despite the prolonged separation, when we initially reunited with Cleo at LAX, it was as if no more than a few hours had passed. Cleo reacted with all the puppy dog glee and energetic enthusiasm that had become her trademark through the years.

It was quite remarkable, really. On the drive home from the airport, she seemed determined to spread the love, rotating between my lap and Candice's every five minutes or so, lapping up kisses whenever she could get a lick in. A few hours later, it was literally as if no time at all had passed. Cleo followed us around the temporary town house we had rented, planting herself beside me as I watched TV or as Candice lay on the couch reading. Being that she had never lived in this new apartment, it was quite amazing just how fast she seemed to get comfortable with it. She had in fact made the platitude that much more crystal clear: Her graceful acclimation to our new physical space seemed directly connected to our being together. She had scoped out the place, figured out where we had put her bowls for food and water—but to her those seemed only the superficial guideposts. Where Candice and I were was where she was most at home.

Within a few weeks, Candice and I also got more comfortable back "at home." We found a house (a few blocks from my sister), laid down every last penny we had for the down payment, and moved in. With the house in tow, Candice got in full nesting mode, settling the place, and within a few more weeks she was pregnant.

√ *Forgiveness* seems like a clunky term in this case because it implies a certain amount of hurt feelings or betrayal that needs to be overcome. Cleo demonstrated no such signs. Her welcoming us back into her life with open paws not only allayed our fears, in hindsight I realized it actually paved the way for a truly transformative life stage. Whatever nervousness we had brought back with us from India, whatever ambiguity around our fortunes (cemented by the Nadi astrologers) was embedded in us, Cleo seemed to calm.

Her graceful acceptance of having us back and her confidence in us that no matter what, we would take care of her, inspired a sense of confidence that spontaneously manifested itself in the ensuing weeks and months.

To that extent, Cleo's forgiving non-forgiveness was so unhuman-like that it made me respect her in an entirely new way. She seemed to embody a set of qualities that were beyond admiration and aspiration. She was so beyond the petty emotions of ordinary human beings, our delicate feelings of abandonment and hurt. She was detached from the emotionalism that gave rise to suffering and yet at the same time, she showed a deep emotional connection to those she loved most—namely Candice and me. All together, this skillful braid of qualities was almost divine-like, something Buddha would be proud of. Maybe my cantankerous old Nadi astrologer wasn't that far off.

Forgiveness is a pretty simple word and the concept behind it easily understood. And yet the components that make it up are various, and the act of forgiveness is perhaps one of the most challenging for humans to undertake.

"Patience, empathy, tolerance, grace, admiration, and compassion—those are just a few of the qualities that form the ribbon of forgiveness. Often those we love most are the hardest to forgive," Papa proposed. We were halfway across the small neighborhood park that sits between our house and Starbucks. Cleo yanked on her leash, poking her nose into the grass where an early morning dew shined. Up ahead, Krishu spotted a few ducks up and at it early, sitting in the pond.

"Ducks, Papa!" A wide smile spread across his face.

I nodded and turned to my father, informing him that we needed to stop for a few minutes so Krishu could watch the ducks, a favorite pastime of his. He shrugged and consented, so the three of us took a seat on a bench beside the pond. Cleo circled and sat by my feet.

Papa picked up where he had previously left off. "The nuances of human relationships, the constant contextualizing of every moment as it relates to some prior or future one, the analytics of our interactions, make the act of forgiveness monumental at times."

Cleo's relationships, on the other hand, with those whom she loved, were pretty straightforward. As her love was unconditional toward those she considered part of her circle, the act of forgiveness came easily to her. As much as it might be her instinct to mark her territory when we went out for her walk, it seemed just as intrinsic to her to forgive those whom she loved.

This, of course, was not a spontaneous nor distinctive characteristic of Cleo's, but rather one that, upon some research, was clearly bred into her through generations' worth of evolution.

In early civilizations, only certain dogs qualified as candidates to be domesticated and brought into settlements and homes. These dogs were the ones that not only proved helpful, submissive, and protective, but most importantly were calm and friendly around their keepers (and their children). If these ancient dogs served as the starting point, the vast majority descended from them, bred through the centuries until today, only served to refine these qualities, making them more tame and more lovable. It was simple natural selection.

Ironically, whereas the original wolves from which dogs are genetically descended were instinctively pack animals, hunters, and predators in order to survive, today's dogs are for the most part anything but. In other words, this whole "man's best friend" thing has literally changed the biology and physiology of our dogs.

Today's socialized dogs like Cleo are physiologically hardwired to love and forgive those they are bonded to. The study of dogs also tells us that the more they socialize or play with their owners—especially at an early age (both the dogs and the owner)—the more their bond is cemented for life.

"In other words," Papa said as he leaned back on the park bench, "Cleo's behavior toward Krishu—her ability to forgive and forget—is a biological characteristic, not just a behavioral one."

I nodded hesitantly. Was this how Watson and Crick contemplated the double helix?

We humans are complicated animals. For better or worse, our wiring is a lot more sophisticated than dogs'. It's what makes us human, after all. So the question of whether or not we are capable of the same instinctive, biological ability to forgive, forget, and reconcile is certainly debatable.

Take for example, I proposed to Papa, what was unfolding in North Korea. The whole dance between Washington and Pyongyang appeared so staged and choreographed, insincere, the cynic would suggest. In the coming hours as the news actually broke and the world started to see images of former president Clinton enduring ceremonies and rituals in North Korea meant to satisfy Kim Jong-il's craving for acknowledgment and attention, a clear impression came across. These were formalities that masked the frosty relationship that preceded President Clinton's visit and that would most certainly remain after he left. It felt like the exact opposite of the type of instinctive emotion we had just been discussing in regard to Cleo and her other canine brethren.

"Well," Papa countered, "there's a lot of value to ritual, actually. The point of all rituals is to capture a certain state of consciousness. Weddings and funerals, bar mitzvahs, Indian thread ceremonies, and thousands of other religious rituals are meant to isolate specific moments and invoke a certain atmosphere and holiness. Ritual often sparks a process that can either trigger healing or formalize a new life stage. Ritual is in fact a powerful part of human civilization, even if it feels formal and insincere at times."

We humans, of course, can be the masters of insincerity and can take our rituals to the most lofty of heights. When it comes to the notion of forgiveness, we've created national debates that have lasted generations as to whether or not our president should formally apologize to the descendents of Native Americans whose predecessors were robbed of their land and worse. In places like South Africa, "truth and reconciliation commissions" have been set up to acknowledge and address the dark legacy of apartheid. In other words, forgiveness and reconciliation does not come easy to us, if only because the crimes that we can commit against one another can cut so deep and wound so gravely.

"And yet still," Papa said, "we can never stop aspiring to be greater, can we?"

"Dada, look!" Krishu pulled on Papa's sleeve. A white swan lolled into the water, slipping between the other less graceful ducks. On the contrary, no matter how many times Krishu had indulged in this ritual in his two years—watching the swans and ducks at the park—it always seemed to spark the same genuine euphoria in him.

"Wow," Papa exclaimed, now having gotten the hang of reciprocating Krishu's enthusiasm after several weeks with him. "Should we go closer?"

Krishu's eyes widened with disbelief. He clutched his dada's hand and hopped from the bench, pulling Papa toward the ducks as if to ensure that Papa would not change his mind.

I sat back and watched the two of them. Cleo looked toward me, seeking guidance if we were staying or going. There were times that chasing ducks and swans and pigeons around parks could fill up entire days for her. These days, by six a.m. she was already looking for her first reprieve from activity. She settled back down beside my feet, happy to wait out Papa and Krishu's playtime before heading off to Starbucks and back home.

Then again, I thought to myself, looking down at her and then over to Papa and Krishu frolicking by the edge of the pond, wherever this ragtag group was, for me really was home.

nine

So, Papa—what is the meaning of life?

The meaning of life is the progressive expansion of happiness. It is to harmonize the elements and forces of our own being with the elements and forces of the cosmos so that we participate in its future evolution of creativity, insight, imagination, infinite possibilities, and also the qualities that we most long for: love, compassion, joy, kindness, equanimity.

Most people have a deep yearning at some stage of their life to seek out the meaning, significance, and purpose of their existence, to understand the deepest mysteries of the universe. I like to think that even seeking the answers to those powerful questions, the process of that exploration, has its own deeper meaning. I know for me it has been that way.

EARLY MORNING PHONE CALLS CAN SPELL BAD NEWS. NOT this one. "Great news," Mom said over the crackling line. "Nana is doing much better. He's asking about everyone."

Great news indeed. Nana's inquisitiveness was back. I could think of no better indication of his recovery.

"He asked me what you were working on," my mother said. "So I told him."

"Yeah." I kind of cringed. "So what did he think of that?"

"He wondered what you could possibly write about that 'half-mad' dog." She laughed. "His words, not mine."

"Half-mad" is a uniquely Indian expression. "Half-*anything*," in fact. "Half-baked," "half-cooked," "half-thought." It was a glorious term, because while "half" of something suggests a portion of the whole—that someone who's half-mad would not, theoretically, be as crazy as someone who is "fully mad"—the "half-mad" person in Indian-speak is actually *totally* nuts, maybe even two times as crazy. Crack that nut if you can.

Nana considered most of the Western hemisphere half-mad. When Mallika and I were younger and Nana and Nani used to travel and stay with us, Nana would shake his head at the way Americans dressed—teens in torn jeans, girls in short skirts, men with earrings (myself included)—and dismiss the whole lot as "half-mad." America was a curious land, a mishmash of strange customs, traditions, rituals, and oddly outfitted citizens.

And then there were our dogs. Nana's experience with dogs was pretty much limited to Nicholas—not the best representative of his species. Nicholas's anarchic temperament ran contrary to the qualities that Nana, a former member of the Indian airforce, held in high regard. If discipline, focus, and structure were things that Nana valued, then Nicholas, and subsequently Cleo, stood in defiant opposition in pretty much every way. Much like my father, Nana was convinced that he could train Nicholas to be a submissive and disciplined dog. Nicholas, of course, proved him wrong with all the sound and fury he could muster.

When Nana caught a fleeting view of Cleo's wild ways, he concluded it wasn't even worth his time and effort to try to harness her. Seeing the way she barked and howled when anyone came home, running laps around the house, dashing in and out of every room (stopping, occasionally, to mark her territory), it was at this stage that he initially invoked the term "half-mad." If the shoe fits . . .

Nana valued the great heroic dogs heralded through history. On the silver screen, probably the most famous was Lassie. Who can forget when the loyal canine alerted the sheriff that little Timmy had fallen down the well? Or how about Laika, the Soviet husky mix that was the first animal to enter orbit when it went up in space aboard Sputnik 2? If ever there was a communist worth emulating, it was that interplanetary pooch. And what about presidential dogs, notably President Clinton's Lab Buddy, who had to live up to his name during the president's darkest hours. Man's best friend indeed.

And then there are those fantastical mutt myths that lead owners like me to believe that dogs like Cleo should have Jedi-like intuition. You know, the ones that sense things like earthquakes, fires, hurricanes, and tsunamis, skillfully warning their masters of the impending dangers? Fortunately for Cleo—in case she ever had any issues of self-esteem—she showed no desire to live up to these lofty standards. She's content in her antihero status. Never once has she alerted us to a forest fire or earthquake. Her sense of people is equally unrefined. While she shows a remarkable capacity to recognize family, even those remote members we see only now and again, pretty much everyone else falls into a collective bucket marked *stranger*. It doesn't matter whether it's a friend, neighbor, delivery man, or cable guy, if you're not family you're a stranger—an interloper, really—and treated to Cleo's particular brand of hostility. Ready. Aim. Bark.

Candice and I have adjusted to this as we have to the rest of Cleo's eccentricities. We've built a veritable sanctuary in the back of the house, outfitting our master bedroom with a plush dog bed, a range of toys, food, and water bowl. Cleo is remanded to this area whenever someone visits the house, our own little madwoman in the attic.

Even with all that, Candice and I knew a new challenge loomed when she became pregnant. As both of us worked considerable hours, we'd need someone to care for our little one, to look after her needs, bathe and clean up after her, and make sure she was also fed. Oh, and she would need to be good with the baby too.

We had to find a nanny. This, of course, meant bringing a non-family member into the house, someone we not only trusted with our child, but who could also coexist with Cleo. I dubbed the mission "Operation Neo" after Keanu Reeves's role in the film *The Matrix*.

Still, it was Candice who was the leader of this mission, if for no other reason than leaving it to me would have led to inevitable disaster. I had tipped her off when I brought up the idea of the Swedish au pair, a strategy I had employed to relieve me of any responsibility. Candice, meanwhile, had more constructively employed a variety of meaningful strategies, from signing us up to nanny search services, to networking with friends and colleagues, to showcasing her protruding belly at the local park, where the powerful nanny cabal hung out daily. Early on, it appeared that this might in fact be the most effective technique. For the word was out and the nannies came a'knocking.

It quickly became apparent to us that many of today's prospective nannies do their own due diligence prior to interviewing. One woman, a fifty-ish immigrant with a narrow face and grand-motherly glasses, had apparently made the Chopra connection. As a result, she armed herself with a definitive strategy: Our child would be exposed only to vegan foods, no sugars, artificial sweet-eners, and a litany of other selective ingredients. Television, video games, even certain types of music would be exorcised from the premises. Cleaning supplies that she concluded had toxic ingredi-ents? Start the bonfire.

Another prospective nanny, cheerful and plump, came dressed in traditional Indian garb (she was Honduran), removed her shoes, and greeted Candice and me with clasped hands and a "namaste."

Still another candidate canceled last minute on Candice because an audition at the same time of our scheduled meeting came through. I guess we should have known something was up when her résumé came with a stylized headshot. Josanna, a pleasant Brazilian woman, brought her ten-year-old niece as a translator, which might have been okay had the girl been able to speak English. And finally there was the woman who halfway through our otherwise not so alarm-ing interview became distraught when she received a call on her mobile phone alerting her that her brother had been shot in Cuernavaca when a "business deal went bad." Very bad.

In this way, we ripped through almost a dozen interviews. Candice and I played along, firing off the questions Candice had scripted, and then nodding along interestedly even as we exchanged glances, raised eyebrows, or scowls. Cleo, meanwhile, had been remanded to her back room sanctuary, her muffled barks forming a steady, if not curious soundtrack to our fruitless process. We rea-soned that unless a candidate was able to impress the two of us, what really was the point of subjecting them to Cleo's wrath?

"You have a dog?" one candidate inquired.

"Yes." I nodded wearily.

"Her name is Cleo." Candice filled the dead space.

"She has very much energy." The woman smiled awkwardly.

I shrugged sheepishly, not sure what to say.

"She's very big?" This last question was accompanied by a nervous smile.

Things were looking entirely wayward when Rosalita entered our house. Unlike many of the others, Rosalita had a confidence about her that was magnetic and encouraging. She was charming, complimenting Candice on her complexion and earning a smile from her that I hadn't seen in precisely seven months. Rosalita was fluent in both English and Spanish (one of our secret hopes for our son) and answered all of Candice's trick questions with precisely the right mix of thoughtfulness and spontaneity. To top it off, she carried a modest-sized binder that contained a number of very strong recommendations from former employers, agencies, and mentors.

Rosalita had run our gauntlet with the same finesse a seasoned Hollywood starlet shows on the red carpet, saying all the right things with just enough variation that they didn't feel scripted, smiling but not posing, and pausing once in a while to intimate serious contemplation on important issues, like at what point an infant should be forced to give up his pacifier. Still, despite all of this, Candice and I knew there was a final test she had to endure. We exchanged a nervous glance and I nodded, excusing myself to retrieve Cleo. I emerged from the back of the house with dog in tow, tightly grasping her leash as she lunged forward, barking up a racket directed at our guest. By this time, of course, the roles were reversed. Candice and I were the ones seeking to impress Rosalita and downplay our nutty dog so as not to ruin our chances with our Neo.

"She's really sweet," Candice yelled over Cleo's incessant barking. "She just needs to get to know you!"

Even as Candice did her best spin, I could feel things slipping away. But Rosalita once again met this challenge head-on, demonstrating tremendous grace under fire. Bending down onto a knee, she reached into her purse and pulled something from it. Holding whatever it was in her clasped palm, she sought permission from us to offer Cleo a treat. Candice nodded with nervous attention and the two of us watched as Rosalita turned her palm and opened it with all the elegance of David Copperfield.

A sucker for anything she might possibly ingest, Cleo quieted down. She knew the drill; it was often the only way to settle her down.

"Come here, Cleo," Rosalita beckoned in just the perfect tone and tenor. Nervously, I loosened my grip on Cleo's leash, allowing her to move forward.

"Don't worry, Señor Chopra," Rosalita assured me. "It's okay."

I let Cleo's leash go limp and she skipped across the room, coming to a graceful stop by Rosalita's feet, sitting obediently there as if the woman were a long-lost aunt. Candice and I both stared speechlessly at what was playing out before us. Who was this imposter of a dog that had impersonated our dear Cleo?

Even as we continued to gawk, Cleo took the treat from Rosalita, scarfed it down, and then licked the hand that fed her affectionately.

We continued to talk, Rosalita sharing more about her own large family in Mexico. Her anecdotes of enormous weddings, festive holiday meals, litters of young kids running around relatives' houses resembled uncannily what both Candice and I were familiar with in our own respective big fat Asian families. The conversation flowed easily, further cementing what Candice and I already knew—that we had found our Neo. Cleo sat calmly and submissively by Rosalita's feet. As she smiled and laughed with us, Rosalita had one hand on Cleo, stroking her belly. By all appearances, Cleo too had found her Neo.

I had become accustomed to wrapping up these interviews in no more than twelve minutes, but remarkably as I looked at my watch, I noticed almost a full hour had passed. Rosalita too looked surprised and rose to her feet, saying she was late for another appointment—changing the course of mighty rivers or scaling tall buildings in a single bound, no doubt. We exchanged good-byes, my promising to be in touch with her shortly so we might formalize things. She nodded bashfully, saying what an honor it would be to work for us.

After shaking my hand, Rosalita turned to Candice, asking sweetly if it was okay to hug her instead of shaking her hand.

"In my family," she said with a smile, "it is good luck to touch a pregnant woman because they are the most precious beings on the Earth."

Candice beamed even more brightly than before and opened herself up for a big hug.

That's when the shit hit the fan.

As Rosalita went in for her hug, Cleo absolutely lost it. As if she had been planning her war strategy in some silent Napoleonic fashion, Cleo didn't just go at Rosalita directly, she leaped from the floor to the couch, vaulting herself off the leather surface and landing like a crazed animal with her paws and teeth embedded deeply into the woman's blouse. Panicked, Rosalita swung from side to side but Cleo held on like a champ, snarling and clawing with a ferocity I'd never seen in her.

Rosalita tried frantically to dislodge Cleo as I did my best to wrestle Cleo from her. But the pup was undeterred and ripped through the woman's silky blouse, shredding it, really, as if it were a highly classified document that needed to disappear. At long last when I was able to finally rip Cleo away, she once again squirmed out of my grasp and went back for more, snapping at Rosalita's stockings, riddling them with tiny teeth marks.

By now, Rosalita was absolutely terrorized, spinning in circles, swatting her arms as if she were being attacked by a swarm of bees, all the while screaming a string of obscenities. She staggered toward the door as I finally wrangled Cleo once more and held her pulsing frame tightly against my chest. Without looking back, Rosalita fled out the door and scrambled down the street, no doubt signaling to the neighbors that our house was the one with the poltergeist in it.

We were devastated. Candice and I both collapsed onto the couch. Cleo, meanwhile, having just recovered her poise, snuggled up to Candice as if nothing at all had happened.

"What the hell are we going to do?" I asked what we were both thinking.

Candice stared at me blankly and sobbed, a reaction I had become accustomed to over the last few months but still didn't have the first clue on how to manage.

"Don't worry." I changed course as abruptly as possible. "We'll figure it out."

I eyed Cleo wearily. Figuring *it* out might mean figuring *her* out.

It was time to confront reality. Cleo was Cleo: She had never shown an aptitude for befriending strangers, and as she got older, things would only get worse. Gradually we started to think the unthinkable—sending Cleo back to live with Candice's mother. It would only be temporary, we rationalized. Just until the baby arrived. Just until we'd found a nanny and things settled down. We'd figure out how to reintegrate her back into the house. Everything would be fine.

Yeah, right.

We both knew that any such move would likely be permanent. Cleo herself was showing signs of aging and it was plain to see. Shipping her around the country, getting her used to new climates (the humidity of the South vs. the dryer air of California) and different surroundings was unlikely and unfair. If she was going, she was likely going for good. We knew that.

For the time being, Candice and I determined the best thing to do was to press pause on our nanny search and any plans to exile Cleo just yet. Our anxiety, of course, was elsewhere. Rosalita might have been injured or badly traumatized, or worse. So Candice called one of the places of reference that Rosalita had listed in her binder. More than anything she was simply looking to broaden the context some, get a better sense if we had any real reason to worry.

The first number appeared to be some sort of placement agency. Its generic name seemed innocuous enough and when the call went to a recording that indicated that the main contact number had changed—though the recording didn't offer a new number—Candice just shrugged it off. But then as she skipped through the list placing calls to some of the other references, similarly odd things persisted. Contact numbers had either changed but offered no forwarding information, were disconnected, or were just plain wrong. In the one instance she did connect with yet another nondescript agency, it took a few moments for the woman on the other end to fully register what Candice was asking for. When at last she understood, she did in fact offer a glowing endorsement of Rosalita. Candice thanked the woman and hung up the phone with a furrowed brow. Something didn't feel right.

"Try one of the personal recommendations," I suggested, sensing something fishy myself.

Candice dialed and waited. A moment later a woman named Leslie picked up on the opposite end.

Hesitantly Candice said that she was calling for a reference check on Rosalita.

"Who?"

Candice explained.

"That's so strange," Leslie responded after a beat.

It was strange because Leslie had had a similar experience with a prospective nanny candidate named Marianna. Marianna, as it turns out, had also left a list of references that was proving nearly impossible to follow up on and validate. Similar to Rosalita, Marianna had met all the other criteria perfectly and also charmed Leslie and her husband, who were looking for someone experienced and caring to look after their son, Beau. Still, Leslie claimed that even before the troublesome reference checks, a "sixth sense told her something was off."

Sadly, neither Candice nor I could really claim the same thing.

Now that we were sufficiently suspicious, we turned up the heat *Law & Order* style. Along with Leslie, our freshly minted joint task force got the goods on Rosalita/Marianna. The woman, it turned out, was a seasoned con artist with a criminal record. With a few even more gullible victims than us, she had managed to finagle advance payments, claiming various hardships, and then skipped out on them. Fortunately none of our digging concluded anything more serious than that. Because obviously when it came to handing one's children over to caretakers, there was the potential for a lot worse.

I chose to look at this event with a glass-half-full disposition. We'd dodged a bullet by not getting ensnared in Rosalita's wily trap. Candice, on the other hand, fell back on the glass-half-empty point of view. She was deeply disturbed we had misread Rosalita so significantly. Our only consolation was the discovery of Cleo's sixth sense. Sure she couldn't differentiate between the garbage truck rolling through the alleyway outside or the destructive gusts of a tempest like Hurricane Katrina, but now we could reasonably argue she might be able to smell out a rat. (Metaphorically speaking, that is, since there was the one time we had a dead mouse in our house for over a week and Cleo failed to detect it.)

Still, Candice—having just hit her eighth month of pregnancy—was spooked enough by the episode that we put our search on hold. Happily for Cleo, largely because she had earned her stripes by being the only one to sense Rosalita's deviousness, this put to final rest any discussion of her shipping out.

With our nanny mission pending, I drifted back into my prior paranoia of whether or not I was truly prepared to be a father. Watching Candice's belly grow was like watching the sand from an hourglass slowly slip away. I knew my days as a carefree guy who still considered himself a kid were numbered and that soon enough there would be a living, breathing being who would happily remind me of that every second of every day. Amid this state of baseline panic, as it turns out though, I was not the only one who noticed Candice growing. A colleague of hers in his infinite observational acumen noticed that Candice was about to pop, and mentioned that a very good friend of his was about to part ways with the woman who had helped raise their son from infancy into his teens. They had adored her so much that they ended up retaining her for years even though they didn't really need her anymore. At one point, their son was out of the house so much that they actually bought a dog to keep the nanny company. Candice and I concluded that the anecdote was cute enough that it should at least earn the prospective candidate an interview.

Candice and I were wary from the start, so we poked around

into this newest candidate's background. Her name was Mirna. She was of Guatemalan origin, had lived in the United States for over a decade, and was keen to keep working so she could support her twenty-year-old son, who was in medical school back home. This heartwarming tale immediately set off alarms for me as I cynically contemplated questions to collapse her story. Candice meanwhile had tears in her eyes. For both Mirna's own good—and more importantly my own—I decided to hold back on the old Gitmo routine. A great thing, in fact, because over the next hour Mirna thawed us out with her warm and genuine affection. She confessed her own misgivings about working for anyone after her last employers, whom, she said, she regarded as family. She was nervous about whether or not she could ever build as close a bond with anyone else, and yet she knew that raising another boy was the only thing that would give her fulfillment.

"How do you know it's a boy?" Candice laughed, her emotionalism having receded.

"I don't know." Mirna shook her head. "Just a feeling, I guess."

At this stage my own feelings were so tangled with emotion, self-doubt, paranoia, and wariness that I knew my best bet was simply to align myself with my wife. I shot Candice a glance and she nodded silently back at me. I knew what this meant. I excused myself to go retrieve Cleo. In a few minutes I returned with her in my hands. I held on to her leash tightly and let her down to the floor. Mirna stared at her a little nervously as Cleo started up barking and lurching toward her.

Mirna didn't have any treats with her nor any other choreographed routine, but clearly she had something else, because as I let her leash go limp, Cleo skipped excitedly toward her and sat by her feet. This time, Cleo didn't go down or roll over, or do anything that remarkable, in fact. On the contrary, she remained just as enthusiastic and giddy as before. She sat for a moment, then leaped to her feet and danced around as if she were doing a Tony Robbins firewalk. Mixed between louder splintered barks, she whimpered excitedly and lurched back and forth and side to side. Candice and I exchanged glances once more. We knew what we were watching: family. "Is she always like this?" Mirna asked a bit hesitantly.

"Yes!" Candice and I exclaimed gleefully at the same time.

MIRNA HAS BEEN with us since the very beginning of Krishu's life. Every morning when she arrives, Cleo goes into the same sort of energetic spasm and dances around in circles like a baby on Red Bull until Mirna settles her down with a treat (or three or four). Krishu, likewise, regards Mirna as family and the three of them communicate almost exclusively in Spanish. Both Candice and I were adamant that Mirna speak in her native tongue to Krishu, hoping he would take to it along with English, Mandarin, and Hindi if he were exposed to it from the earliest stage. What we weren't expecting was that Cleo would go Spanish on us as well. Then again, we could hardly claim surprise when Cleo once more defied expectations.

Like many people in our lives, Mirna was at first a little awed by my father. While she hadn't read any of his books, she was aware of who he was and initially reacted nervously when he dropped in to see his grandchildren. One afternoon after he had dropped by, played with Krishu for a few minutes, and then slipped outside to use his cell phone, Mirna pulled me aside and urged me to advise her in the future when my father was coming so that she could adequately prepare Krishu.

"What do you mean?" I asked her, unclear what it meant for Krishu to be "prepared."

She insisted that Krishu be fully napped, cleaned up, bathed, dressed appropriately, his hair combed and fingernails clipped if he was going to meet his grandfather.

I assured her that all of that was not necessary. But she pushed back in a way that showed she meant business. Twenty minutes later, he emerged from his room looking like a dolled-up choirboy. Twenty minutes after that, he stood stiffly in front of my father, who stared awkwardly at his comb-over.

"What happened to him?" Papa asked.

I shook my head and then smiled at Mirna, who beamed with pride.

Fortunately for us all, within another twenty minutes Krishu was rubbing banana bread in his hair and the planet was happily back on its axis.

Gradually as the months passed, Mirna got more comfortable around my father. Still, she insisted that whenever Krishu was to spend time with my father, he was prepped and rested for it. She even chided Papa once or twice for daring to look at his BlackBerry when he was supposed to be focused on his grandson. In part, Mirna's desire for Krishu and my father to have a strong bond was linked to her awareness of Papa's celebrity—she wore my father's connection like a proud badge, especially around her cronies at the local park. But really it was her own cultural heritage that held sacred the bond between men in a family.

"To be a good man, Krishu must know good men," she told me once.

It sounded like a reasonable covenant to me and I nodded my approval of it.

"Now, if you and your father want to be great men," she continued, fueled by my endorsement, "you will learn from your son just how to be."

This time I stared at her, unsure what she meant. Had I lost something in the translation? She smiled back at me, pleased with herself. It became clear to me that pressing her most likely would not yield the clarity I was seeking. I let it go.

Over the course of the last few months, as my father started to spend days if not a week at a time with us, Mirna, of course, noticed. She inquired with Candice if everything was fine at home, presumably between my parents. We had learned over the years that casually relaying information that could easily transform into gossip amongst the nanny cabal at the park was akin to leaving a loaded gun around the house. To ward off any trouble, Candice advised her of my grandfather's health, my mother's prolonged stay in India, and instructions to me to spend more time with my father over the summer.

Mirna nodded knowingly as if she had been let in on some sort of secret. "He should spend more time with the baby and the dog," she unexpectedly advised.

One afternoon she seemed to put this unique prescription into practice. Having been out at a meeting, I returned home to find Mirna standing outside of the house peering in through the blinds. I asked her what was going on.

"Your father." She pointed inside. "He's here."

"Okay." I nodded, unsure if that was the full explanation or not.

"He told me to take the rest of the day off. That he would take care of the baby."

My expression clearly betrayed me.

"Yeah." She nodded. "That's why I stand out here and watch them." She squinted again through the shutters.

"He's actually not so bad," she added.

I moved beside her and peered through the window. Krishu

seemed in heaven. He was holding Papa's hands rotating in a circle. He was one of few children I'd ever seen who drew profound enjoyment from one-on-one ring-around-the-rosy. Unexpectedly, from the looks of my father's expression, he appeared to be just as into it. The moment they "all fell down," Cleo too joined the party, barking up a storm as both Krishu and Papa rolled with laughter.

"I told you." Mirna smiled with a sense of pride. "Krishu and Cleo very good for him. He can write a book about them."

I thanked her and relieved her of her surveillance.

Entering into the house, I now got a broader glimpse of the living room, which couldn't be seen from the outside. In the hour that they had been left alone, Cleo, Papa, and Krishu had wreaked such havoc in the house, it appeared as if a hurricane had flashed through.

"What happened?" I stared around the room like a Red Cross worker who had just arrived on the scene.

"Nothing." Papa shrugged as he crashed to the floor again with Krishu. Riled once more, Cleo danced out of their way, hopped onto the couch, and took out her hyperness on an innocent pillow that she'd already had at. The cotton from inside of it flew while she whipped it from side to side with her jaw. Clearly, while she lacked the capacity to sense a natural disaster, with conspirators like my father and my son, she had no problem making it look like one had occurred.

"Again, Dada!" Krishu sang as he sprang to his feet.

Papa lumbered to his.

The two of them started up again. "I spoke to Mom this morning," Papa said as they made their first turn.

He faced me and grinned broadly. "She's coming home in ten days."

"Down!!!" Krishu bellowed. He often skipped most of the other words in ring-around-the-rosy to get to his favorite part.

Papa tumbled down to the floor once more. "She'll be able to go with us to Whistler."

This was great news. Every summer my family planned a family trip. Over the last few years we hit Colorado and Wyoming and collectively fell in love with the vast landscapes, lazy days, and outdoorsy activities they both offered. This year, we were traveling to Whistler in British Columbia, Canada, where my father was going to be conducting one of his weeklong spiritual seminars. Aside from the fact that we needed to play out the perfectly spiritual family, it seemed another ideal spot for us to continue our annual tradition. I envisioned full days of hiking, mountain biking, maybe even kayaking and fishing if the mood was right. We had all started to confront the reality that my mother was not likely to be back for the trip, which made it far less than ideal.

But the fact that Mom was going to be back in time to join us signified several great things. It not only guaranteed a gleeful reunion for us all, but also meant that Nana's health had improved significantly. It also meant that while on vacation, Candice and I might even have the occasional chance to go out for "adult dinners" while my mom supervised the boy. While we most certainly loved Krishu above all else, the notion of a "date night" had become far more mythic lore than reality in the past two years for us. Add Cleo's increasing need in her old age for walks every few hours, and there was rarely the opportunity for Candice and me to slip out and get away.

Most of all, though, I could tell by looking at my father and the sudden weight that seemed to have been lifted from his shoulders, the news of my mother's imminent return had bolstered him.

Even I often got caught up in the aura that clustered around Papa. It was easy to forget that just like everyone else, the sense of companionship he drew from my mother was special to him. We rarely if ever discussed it, and yet intuitively we all knew it was the glue that held our whole family together, but most of all balanced him.

This time when Papa and Krishu fell to the floor, Cleo joined them. She pranced around Papa, hopping on her hind legs and trying to join in the fun, her tail wagging furiously back and forth.

"You want to hear a bizarre story?" Papa sat back against the couch and laid a hand on Cleo's head.

"I was working out this morning at the gym," he began, "and a woman in pink spandex and sunglasses approached me."

You may think that the lady in pink spandex and sunglasses is bizarre enough, but in the crazy spiritual life of Deepak Chopra, that was par for the course. Often he or we came across strangers who confided in him some of their innermost secrets or thoughts. Once in the Frankfurt airport, in a restroom, a man at the urinal beside my father recognized him, got so excited that he forgot what he was doing, and turned to Papa to tell him how he had dreamed several weeks ago how he would "meet his guru very soon." Whether or not the dream included his urinating on the guru's shoes, we may never really know.

"I believe the karmic significance was the universe telling me to stop wearing alligator-skin shoes," Papa later extrapolated from the strange episode. Ever since, you'll find him mostly in brash red sneakers.

"She was an animal psychic and told me that I had a small fluffy white dog who was very important to my spiritual evolution." As if she could hear him, Cleo lay on the ground, spryly rolled onto her back, spread her legs, and waited to be stroked by Papa. A very spiritual response, of course.

"She said that the dog was reprising a role from a prior life and that I needed to learn from her as much as possible."

It crossed my mind. Might this pink-spandexed, sunglass-clad woman be my editor in disguise? My agent perhaps?

"What do you think?" Papa looked at me.

My father is not a very religious man, despite his notoriety for being one of the most spiritual guys around. If you ask him, he claims to be no more a Hindu (the faith with which he grew up) than a born-again Christian. And yet, as perhaps the world's leading go-to guru on *consciousness*, a lot of what he speaks about and believes is drawn directly from the spiritual traditions of India, known as the Vedas. The notion of reincarnation—that the human body is recycled matter and that what we define as a person and/or personality is nothing more than that same consciousness refashioning itself—is aligned with what many Hindus claim as their faith. For my father, this has been a source of great consternation for years. For what he believes he can (like no other) rationalize and explain through science and modern physics, others believe blindly and fasten to their faith. In many ways, it has undermined his own work and he knows it. Still, the notion that a family unit like ours is not just a random computation of the universe, thrown together indiscriminately for one lifetime, but rather a function of a deeper cosmic intelligence orchestrated by consciousness, or dare we call it God, was not incredulous. If anything, it reaffirmed the instincts that we intuitively felt. The fact that a pink-spandexed doggy psychic might suggest that Cleo was part of our transcendental pack was entirely believable to my father, especially considering their intense summer bond.

"I think Cleo has definitely been around for a few lifetimes," I replied to Papa. "Do you?"

Papa laughed, looking down at Cleo. Krishu pulled at Papa's sleeve, urging him back to his feet. "Again!"

"Yes," Papa said. "I think we've all been around one another a few times. One lifetime wouldn't nearly be enough fun."

WHEN I WAS a child, every so often, Papa used to put Mallika and me to sleep. He wasn't much into reading us stories, or even telling us stories, but rather would encourage us to tell him a story. He had read in one of his countless books that there was nothing more creatively stimulating for children's minds than their creating stories. He encouraged this quality in us and today does the same thing with our children, his grandchildren, notably Tara.

This, of course, has generated some family controversy because Tara's, er, storytelling (aka lying) has proven to be rather prolific. Recently her teachers at school called my sister with some alarm, concerned whether or not on a recent trip to India Tara's family had been attacked by some British hooligans.

"What?" Mallika responded, clearly confused.

Further investigation revealed something quite fascinating. During a recent trip to India, Tara's paternal grandfather took her to the Mahatma Gandhi museum in central New Delhi to show her some of the history around India's struggle for independence from the British. The museum sits on the plot of land where Gandhi was actually assassinated by an Indian gunman, in large part because the assassin disagreed with Gandhi's peaceful resistance to the British.

It appeared that Tara had taken this emotional journey into her own ancestral history and wrapped it around a more modern tale in which a fictional rowdy British mob attacked her family.

Mallika assured Tara's teachers that no such incident had occurred.

"Good," the teacher replied. "Then I assume your in-laws' elephant is okay as well?"

Mallika laughed along with Tara's teacher. "Fortunately the elephant is okay."

Of course, Mallika considered this to be no laughing matter. She addressed it with my father at dinner one night. Perhaps it was not such a good idea for him to continue encouraging Tara's storytelling skills.

"Nonsense," he responded defiantly. "We should absolutely encourage it! We should nurture it."

He looked at Tara proudly. She sat with a conflicted expression, half-embarrassed at being caught in her lie, half-proud of her grandfather's admiration. Cleo sat dutifully by her feet, curiously with almost the same expression, I thought.

"Tara may be the next Steven Spielberg. Or Jhumpa Lahiri."

"Or James Frey," I added.

Papa continued. "Storytelling is how we package our intuition. It means she's tapped in. It's marvelous, actually."

Tara's smile widened. She was definitely more proud now than embarrassed.

It was funny how things reprised themselves. I remembered some form of this same debate between my mom and dad when I was young and he encouraged Mallika's and my storytelling skills. I stretched this as far as I could over the years, once telling my parents as a teen after a boozy night out with my friends that I was under the impression I'd been drinking "Arnold Palmers" and not Long Island iced teas.

"Like the baseball player?" my father asked, perplexed. (He never cared much for sports.)

My mom ordered me to bed to sleep it off. "Speaking of Arnold Palmer, don't count on getting much more than a golf cart when you get your driver's license next year."

This, of course, just added to my father's confusion.

Years later, now Mallika was playing the role of my mom, showing concern that Tara's creative storytelling skills today might transform into something more menacing and difficult to handle tomorrow when she hit her teens.

"Papa!" Mallika shot my father a look. This time Mallika was not reprising anything. Looking at her, she *was* my mother and Papa knew it. Mallika didn't need to say anything more.

"Okay," he relented. He turned to Tara. "Maybe school isn't the best place to tell your stories," he advised her.

That was the best Mallika could have hoped for. There was no way she would convince him that creativity was not the source of all problem solving in the world. Even she had to remember that when we were small he told us that there was nothing unreal about what happened in our dreams, or any memories we claimed to have of lives before this one.

"The only thing not real," he told us when we were still in elementary school, "is the socially induced hallucination that *this* is all there is."

Yes, ladies and gentlemen, I grew up in the Matrix.

There was one particular memory from my days of storytelling as a child that I recalled in light of Papa's encounter with the pink-spandexed woman at the gym. After dinner and the chilled conversation between Papa and Mallika, I reminded him of it.

"Remember the dream I once told you about where you and I met on a rope bridge in China?"

"Yes," Papa said without even pausing. "You had a dog with you."

It's true. In the dream, we were two peasants, but I was older and he was younger. We were strangers to each other except for that single encounter on a rope bridge that connected two peaks in a mountainous range in China. I had a dog with me and he had a bowl of rice with him. On the bridge, Papa offered me some of his rice and as we sat and ate, we shared our life stories. He was a tea trader who regularly traversed the country from the foothills of Bhutan to the ports of the South China Sea. I was a calligrapher whose services were once sought by aristocrats in big cites, but who now preferred to teach children from rural towns.

At the end of our encounter, I told Papa that I needed to go and that I wanted him to take care of the dog. I explained to him that I was old and didn't have much time left but that the dog had more living to do and needed a companion. He nodded and agreed to take the dog with him.

I thanked him and before we parted, I got on one knee and said an emotional good-bye to the dog.

"It's okay," the young man advised me on that rope bridge between those two mountains in China in *that* life. "We'll all meet again," he said.

"I remember that." Papa nodded his head and we both looked down at Cleo. "So here we are again just like I said we would be."

In my family we have always believed in a deeper karmic connection among us. This is actually not a *belief* among us as much as it is an awareness. We have a lot of fun with one another and have a deep admiration for one another. My sister and her husband's kids are mine and Candice's, and Krishu is theirs. These days Papa often tweets that his grandchildren are the greatest teachers in his life.

With Cleo, watching the way that she interacts with family, even remote members or those she somehow identifies as family, like Mirna, as opposed to how she reacts to everyday strangers, reenforces the suspicion that she's been hanging with us multiple lifetimes. More than just the fun we have together, it's in fact all of the qualities that she's shown to us over the years—her devotion and trust, loyalty, unconditional love, nonjudgment, and more—that form the mechanics of her self-knowing.

A lot of people are familiar with canine science. They study pack mentality ad nauseam and make heated cases for or against its very existence. They elucidate the fascinating dynamics that link humans and dogs, including the ways in which dogs are able to read even the most subtle gestures, body language, facial expressions, vocal tones, and emotions of their masters.

"But with Cleo," Papa continued as we propelled the conversation forward on our now nightly walk to Starbucks for an after-dinner tea, "you don't have to.

"Simple science—the size of Cleo's tiny head—suggests her brain only has so much capacity. And yet, her emotional resonance with all of us suggests that her intelligence stems from something far more subtle than the brain inside her head. Cleo is *tapped in* in a way that most humans are not, not because they are unable to but because they have reorganized themselves and their instincts to not even see or sense what is right in front of them. She is steered by a higher guidance."

Another revelation for Cleo, I commented as I looked down at her. Indeed she had a skip in her step as we neared the block on which Starbucks sat. Granted, it was most likely due to the piece of cherry Popsicle Krishu dropped after dinner and she managed to inhale before I got to it.

As we reached Starbucks, Papa entered and I grabbed a seat outside with Cleo. She sniffed around on the sidewalk searching for anything interesting as I admired her. It was truly amazing to me how so much of the neuroses we had identified over the years in her could now be transformed into spiritual insight. Perhaps Cleo's greatest gift was that she lacked the anxiety-inducing need to even doubt or analyze her own intuitive sense. She was uniquely focused on only the things important to her—at this moment the half-eaten apple she'd just discovered wedged between the chair and the wall.

Just then a young man exited the Starbucks. He had a goatee and wore a beanie from which a tangle of hair emerged. He laughed as he spoke into his cell phone.

"Hey, you know that guy I told you that was in line in back of me that looked just like Deepak Chopra?" He shook his head incredulously. "It's so funny—I heard him talk and he sounded just like him too!"

ten

If you could do it all over again, what would you do differently?
I wouldn't do any of it differently. That's the truth.
Nothing?
It may turn out differently because I hope I'd do it just as spontaneously as I did it this time around. Most of everything I have this time came effortlessly, not because I wasn't trying or working hard but because I took it for the most part as it came. I believe creativity comes from spontaneity, which I'm pretty good at. Some people call it impulsiveness, but it works for me.

"I FEEL GREAT," NANA ASSURED ME OVER THE PHONE. HE had been home for a few weeks and sounded very much like his old self. He was eager to get back to his routine: going on walks in the park, hanging with his old military cronies, and complaining about Indian politicians. "They're a useless lot," he reminded me.

"Your mother said you're writing a book about that dog of yours," he said.

"Well," I started, ". . . it's really not just about Cleo, but me, my dad, Krishu, and Cleo." Hopefully, the success of the book wouldn't be tied to my ability to sell it to my grandfather.

"Sounds fascinating," Nana replied.

Indifferent? Perplexed? It was hard to fully grasp his tone. "Really?"

"No. Your father writes books about the search for happiness. Your dog—any dog—they are just happy. What else is there to say?"

Indeed.

"Look," he said. "Don't bother sending a new copy of the book when it's done. We'll just get one from the library. You never know how long we'll be around."

"HOW IS HE?" Candice asked as she zipped up a suitcase.

"Totally back to normal." I smiled.

I confronted the four suitcases, three carry-ons, stroller bag, car seat bag, and "miscellaneous bag" she had packed for our trip.

"It's mostly *his* stuff."

She wasn't lying. Between Krishu's clothes, diapers, wipes, foods, toys, books, stroller, car seat, and *miscellaneous* stuff, my twenty-six-pound son apparently required about four times that weight just to keep him functional.

"Hey," Candice cut me off before I could even start, "if you want to go through it all and repack, be my guest."

I shook my head. "I'll pack the car."

The hitch, of course, with going to Canada was Cleo. In years past, we'd taken her with us, even smuggled her into fancy resorts where dogs were outlawed. But this trip bore the "international" stamp, and Cleo was clearly a domestic mutt. I sensed from her the same sentiments I had. Canada was more a cousin than some distant relation and, well, in our family cousins were essentially siblings. But that would hardly fly with the border agents. No doubt about it. Cleo would be staying home.

Our default had always been to leave Cleo with my sister or my mother, but since we were all traveling together this time around, those options were out. So was the long trip to Candice's mom; Cleo was simply too old to endure it. We never even considered leaving her with the local vet, who would keep Cleo in a small cage and give her only two walks a day. And we knew better than to look for a house sitter/dog walker. With Cleo's dynamic mix of unfriendliness and growing neurosis it would be the nanny interviews all over again. As for sending her to someone else's home, well, that would be like asking the neighbor if we could set up a sleeper cell in the living room.

"Take her to one of those fancy doggy day cares," one of Candice's mommy friends advised her over coffee one day. She "bumped" the details of one she recommended from her iPhone to Candice's.

I went online to check it out. The steep price meant if we were to pursue this option, we would become *those* people who spent insane amounts of money to make sure that our dog lived the cushy life. Still, I knew just how to justify it:

Seven nights at doggy day care: $350.
Special low-fat dog food for old bitches like Cleo: $10 a day.
Guilt-free vacation for Gotham and Candice: priceless.

A young woman named Missy led us on a tour of the facility. A spacious play area annexed the bright lobby. Big dogs sprinted in circles playing games with friendly trainers. Separated by a sturdy barrier sat a smaller pen with dogs more Cleo's size lazily lounging around, sniffing each other, and playing with plush toys. Sun poured through big open windows. A fresh breeze ensured that too much of a doggy smell never lurked.

Missy observed me scrutinizing the playpen where presumably Cleo would end up. Never one to really "work a room," Cleo might not cut it with the others, I thought to myself. She really wasn't much of a networker, much more the type to keep her snout to the pavement, and well, keep her snout to the pavement. Missy confirmed that the dogs were given free range in these areas and spent the majority of their days hanging with each other, playing, and wandering around in circles.

"Don't worry," she assured me, "anytime any sort of tension breaks out, we separate them so nothing builds."

In particular, mealtimes were specifically set aside and food was kept in separate areas to avoid skirmishes between the dogs. If Cleo were to stay there, Missy told us, she could expect a private dining period every morning and evening during which a trainer would provide her with personal attention, making sure she got her full meal. Candice and I exchanged glances. Things were looking good.

At night, there was a heavily pillowed area where the dogs lounged out and got their rest. Owners were encouraged to bring unlaundered T-shirts and leave them so that their dogs had something identifiable to lie out on, a reminder of familiar and comforting smells. All in all, our tour did nothing but reassure us that we had at last found the solution to our long-standing problem. Candice in particular was enormously pleased, so we agreed to give it a try. Missy escorted Candice to a private office to fill out some paperwork while I hung back, content to check my iPhone for e-mails and hang by the play area, where a dozen or so dogs were racing back and forth playing.

After a few minutes, a young man entered the room and stood beside me. "What's up, bro?" He gestured toward me with a slight tilt of his chin. It was a "guy greet" and I reciprocated the signal.

"Bro" held about half a dozen leashes, but what got my attention were his heavily tattooed arms. He had what are commonly referred to as sleeves, tattoos covering his arm with no sign of any un-inked skin. Not an inch. He wore a snow hat, a blond goatee, and a T-shirt with STAY SUCKER FREE printed across it.

"My name's Nomi, bro." He stuck out his hand to shake mine.

We exchanged a firm shake.

"One of these yours?" he inquired, gesturing to the dogs in the play area.

"No." I shook my head. "She's coming tomorrow."

"Ah, a bitch." He smiled and nodded. "Like literally, right? What's her name?"

I was taken aback. "Um . . . Cleo."

"Um Cleo or just Cleo?" He laughed. "I'm just playing with you, bro. I'll keep an eye out for Cleo. I walk the boys and girls," he said, and then shook his shoulders and danced to a beat that was nowhere to be heard.

We stood for a moment while I tried to reconcile Nomi with my image of what a dog walker should be.

"You know what this place reminds me of?" Nomi nodded, referring to the play area in front of us.

I shook my head.

"Prison." He smiled. "I mean, not that neither you or me would know what that shit is like, right, bro?" He winked at me and smiled. "Like seriously. Like this is the yard, right?"

My only experience with prison yards (thankfully) were the terrifying MSNBC documentaries I sometimes watched late at night. Even they gave me nightmares.

"Like check it out," Nomi continued. "See when a new dog comes in, they're released into the general population right here. They need to figure out how to play it, you know? Like either they need to just flat out assert themselves, like locate the top dog and just go after that old dog and make it clear who's boss now so all the others know. Or you know, go more covert. Just slip in all Mossad, find your Bloods or Crips and swear allegiance, you know? Just watch my back, right?" He laughed again.

I stared out at the dogs in the play area, my jaw agape.

"Serious, bro, these dogs are amazing, the way they need to organize themselves and figure their shit out and get comfortable with one another. It's like a hierarchy that forms itself, and then keeps on forming itself. It's actually pretty great, bro. Cleo's going to dig it. What's she like?"

I didn't know what to say. All of a sudden I wasn't so sure about this plan, about the yard, and releasing innocent little Cleo into the general population. In fact, in that moment I all but decided to call the whole thing off.

"I don't know really." I shook my head. "I mean, I don't know how she'll do here."

Nomi was opening the door to the play area. The pack of dogs rushed toward him and he stroked them, gently pulling individual dogs toward him, latching the leashes onto their collars as he identified each one of them, Tiger . . . Gypsy . . . Buddy . . . Nelly . . . and more.

When each leash was fastened Nomi gently led the pack from the play area, shutting the door behind them.

"I feel you." He turned to me. He bent down on a knee and carefully picked up one of the dogs. "This is Chaucer. He was just like that."

Chaucer, a little mixed mutt remarkably similar in appearance to Cleo, extended his tongue and licked Nomi's face affectionately. All of a sudden Nomi seemed the most gentle soul on planet Earth. He returned Chaucer's affection and more.

"Chaucer came in all scared and unsure of himself, but by day two he had figured his shit out and he was all John Adams in here, leading the other dogs and trying to draft a bill of rights and shit." Nomi buried his face into Chaucer's and rubbed him lovingly. "Isn't that right, buddy?

"It's all good though." He placed Chaucer down on the ground and turned to me. "I mean, they deserve it, right? Cleo deserves it, right?"

I stared at Nomi, speechless. He was a contradiction in every way. Just then, Candice and Misty emerged from the office. Candice wore a broad smile on her face. "This is going to be really great for her."

"Aw yeah." Nomi introduced himself to Candice. "Cleo's going to find herself here, ma'am.

"Later, bro." He extended his hand and "guy-gripped" mine, then gave me a hug like we were boys from the hood.

OUR JOURNEY TO WHISTLER, a scenic ski town a two-hour drive north of Vancouver, was remarkably and spectacularly uneventful. As had become our custom with Krishu with any instance that required over an hour's worth of focused time in a condensed space like a car, his and our new best friend Dora the Explorer was our trusted companion. Despite our naive insistence that we were going to limit Krishu's TV time, Dora, Diego, Boots, Swiper, and the gang now had a permanent place in our lives. Candice had downloaded several hours' worth of the cartoon onto her laptop, which fit easily in her purse and could be brought out in the blink of an eye. If only the FAA didn't require all electronics to be shut down for takeoff and landing, we would have accomplished our own international nonstop Dora marathon by the time we reached the breathtaking peaks of Whistler.

The moment after check-in, before even going to our own room, we rushed to my parents' suite. They had arrived a few hours earlier and were already settled. We had all been curious to see how Krishu would react after having not seen my mom for several months. This was a wild card in his young life.

Prior to her leaving for India, she had a firm grip on his devotion. Only Candice topped her in his hierarchy of affection. Even I sat on a decidedly lower perch, outranked by my nieces, Tara and Leela, who held a special place in Krishu's heart. Papa, meanwhile, had made significant strides over the last few weeks, earning a prominent stature in Krishu's life. What would happen now that my mother had returned was anybody's guess. I suspected that he secretly hoped Krishu would demonstrate their bond in front of my mom, so he could openly gloat about it.

"Dadi!!!!" Krishu yelled the moment he laid eyes on my mom. He rushed toward her and crashed into her legs with unfiltered affection. My mother could barely get his name out before she broke into tears, a torrent of emotion unleashed. Krishu climbed into her lap and urged her, "Don't cry. Be happy!"

"Are you Dada's baby?" Papa inquired a few minutes later when things settled down.

Krishu smiled with his eyes, mischief spreading across his face. "No, Dadi's baby!"

Papa prodded him again. "Dada's baby?"

"No, Dadi's baby!!" Krishu insisted.

"I have a Popsicle." Papa raised his eyebrows, resorting to trickery.

Krishu's eyes widened with excited curiosity.

"Do you want it?" Papa slowly reeled him in.

"You know you'd better have a Popsicle," I interrupted them.

Papa shot me a look of confusion.

"You do have a Popsicle, don't you, Papa?" Candice pressed.

Papa's smile flattened. "Oh shit."

My mom, Candice, and I shook our heads in unison.

"Popsicle?" Krishu hadn't caught on yet. He climbed out of my mom's lap and marched toward Papa.

"I'll take him right now to find a Popsicle," Papa assured us.

I shrugged. Why not, I thought. I was keen to take a shower and Candice wanted to check out the hotel spa. While either one of us could easily have pulled a bait and switch on the kid, we wanted Krishu to know that his grandfather lived up to his word. Papa swept Krishu up into his arms and carried him from the room.

About thirty minutes later I received a nervous call on my cell phone.

"Hi, Gotham." The woman introduced herself as Julie. She was trying to track down my father, who in just minutes was supposed to be welcoming the group. He was nowhere to be found and he wasn't picking up his cell phone either.

"Someone said your father was with your son?" she said hopefully. "Do you know where they might be?"

How was I supposed to respond? Should I confess that my two-year-old had demanded a Popsicle and that in order to maintain the sanctity of their relationship my father had no choice but to canvass the whole Olympic village to find one?

"Um," I said hesitantly. "I'm not really sure."

I promised a slightly panicked Julie I'd get right on it and start the search for my father. In the meanwhile, I advised her to just have the five hundred or so guests meditate. It was an old Chopra fallback. Can't sleep? Meditate. Excessive turbulence on your flight? Meditate. Writer's block? Meditate.

"Good idea," Julie replied, and hung up the phone.

About fifteen minutes later, after the all-points bulletin had gone out for Papa with the entire Chopra family dispatched in various directions, I found Papa sitting with Krishu on a bench in the middle of the Olympic village. When he spotted me, Krishu smiled broadly, grape Popsicle smeared across his face. Papa, though he had managed to maintain a cleaner appearance, licked his own red Popsicle.

"Hi, Papa!" Krishu greeted me.

"Papa," I summoned my father. "What are you doing?"

"Having Popsicles," he announced, waving his cherry-flavored one at me. "I haven't had a Popsicle in probably thirty years."

He stroked Krishu's hair. "I don't know if I've had this much fun in all that time."

I chose not to mention the fact that I was thirty-four years old. I knew where he was coming from.

"Papa—you're late," I said. "Everyone's waiting for you."

He looked at me, perplexed.

"You're supposed to be welcoming the group right now," I informed him.

His expression straightened, though he didn't seem to panic.

"I should get going." Papa got up from the bench.

"I told Julie to have everyone meditate."

He grinned. "That's what I would have done."

"I know." I smiled back at him as I took the seat beside Krishu.

Papa took a step back toward the resort and then stopped. He turned. "If you hadn't come, I think Krishu and I may have sat there forever."

I patted Krishu on the head. "I know. That's what I would do."

FOR YEARS, MY FATHER had been conducting seminars like the one he'd be leading over the next week in Whistler. Some were as short as a weekend and involved groups as small as a dozen, while others, like the Seduction of Spirit, lasted a full week and the number of attendees climbed into the hundreds. The family had attended several of these courses over the years, largely because it enabled us to spend time together in spectacular resorts like the one in Whistler. But there was another factor that was impossible to miss. It was during his courses that Papa was at his best.

For all of his best-selling books, the blogs and articles that appear in the blogosphere, for all the television appearances and celebrity consultations, even the one-night-with-Deepak speech extravaganzas that often left audiences inspired and *spiritualized*, Papa was never *on* the same way he was when he was intensively interacting over the course of a few days with a large number of people like he did on these courses. The mix of personal interactions he provided attendees during private consultations or even when one of them managed to corner him in a hallway, along with his daily addresses to the entire group, fueled him with an energy and buzz that was entirely unique to every other aspect of his life. Even for us—who instinctively humbled him and made sure he never got too lost in his spiritual orbit—seeing Papa in this setting was a reminder of what he did for a living and how powerful it could be for people.

Early one morning, a few days into the course, I found him

down in the gym steadily pacing the treadmill. The fact that he had a coffee in his hands from which he occasionally sipped signaled the intensity of his workout. I was hardly one to talk. While for him a leisurely stroll on the treadmill in the predawn hours was a good escape from the deliberation of the course of which he was at the literal center, for me it was likewise a way to get away from the never-ending child care routine that Krishu demanded.

I climbed atop the treadmill beside Papa and ramped it up. "How's it going?"

"It's going." He smiled. "That's what they say these days, right?"

I nodded back at him. For all of his isolation from modern pop culture—he's walked treadmills beside Britney Spears and Sylvester Stallone and had no idea who they were—he strives to remain plugged in to some of the more relevant elements of the zeitgeist. Technology, social networking, cinema, and language—the ways in which we communicate and learn from one another—are obsessions of his. While I may shudder when he mixes up pop jargon (who can forget "that dope is shit"?), it never stops him from trying.

I asked him about the group.

"They're exceptional," he said admirably. "A really unbelievable group this time."

He took a sip from his coffee. "There's one guy who has created the concept of a 'gift economy.' He and his wife do not use money. They exist by giving their time and effort, and then accepting the gifts and grace of others. It's awesome. There's a lot we could learn and adapt to our own collapsed economy. Imagine if everyone in the world was a little bit more charitable, not with actual money but with service. It would completely transform the planet's economy."

Papa put his coffee down. "There's another woman who's a geneticist. She's one of the foremost experts in the world on gene-mapping. Some of the stuff she was talking about last night was absolutely mind-boggling." He was getting more excited just talking about it. "I mean, where science is going . . ."

He continued. "I've connected her with a guy who's here from France who is one of the architects of the French health-care system. Did you know that their system is considered one of the best in the world?

"I'm having coffee with them later today and another fellow who has successfully started and sold two technology companies for a few hundred million dollars and has now created a new proprietary piece of technology. It's like a widget that anyone can personalize and use as a gateway to cataloging their own personal well-being. I think together the three of them can combine their insights and resources and help solve the health-care crisis in this country."

With all seriousness, Papa turned to me, wagging his finger. "President Obama should actually be here."

My father in a nutshell. A part of him is the eternal optimist. He truly believes that he has a unique ability to connect people from all parts of the planet, mind-meld them, and shift collective consciousness.

He talked about more people, experts in microfinancing, counterterrorism, integrative wellness, cell phone technology, behavioral scientists, child-care psychologists, and more. Some of the terms were so alien to me, I couldn't even compute exactly what they did.

"You know, Gotham"—Papa sipped from his coffee and exhaled with a sense of gravity—"we live in such an amazing age of transformation. Technology will soon enable us to reengineer our bodies and consciousness from our BlackBerrys. The question is whether or not we'll guide ourselves toward that end."

There were times like these that I sensed a deep sense of disappointment and despair from Papa. It was the other dark side of his optimism, the steep drop from having a front row seat to such amazing human potential, and yet sadly knowing that most often our race marshaled those resources to the same old, same old—war and weaponry, privatization and enormous wealth for the very few.

"Yesterday, in one of our group sessions, one of the people said this is the 'age of unboundedness' because of the potential we have with all our technology and resources."

He laughed. "You know what I thought of when she said that? Unboundedness?"

I shook my head. "What?"

"Cleo." He smiled.

Oh boy, had he and Cleo made strides. Not only had he recognized a litany of spiritual qualities in her over the course of the summer, he now thought she was a potential pioneer to lead us into the brave new technological world of the future.

"True unboundedness comes from a sense of pure being. Not from doing or trying, but from just being. It's not about gaining recognition or earning respect. It's not about getting a prize or winning an award or making a dividend, it's about not operating from the ego, offering your self back to everyone else because you know that ultimately even your so-called self is just a recycled piece of the whole. Even you are not yours to begin with—so offering it back is just another exercise in consciousness."

See, I thought to myself, this is what happens after a few days of chronic meditation and spiritual workshopping.

"Cleo is unbounded because she's in touch with her*self* and she knows her*self* is not even her real self."

"Well, we'd better get her a passport then," I joked.

Papa laughed. "Right—maybe instead of Obama, we'd be better off if Cleo had been here."

I CALLED THE doggy day care for daily updates. According to Missy, on days one and two, Cleo largely kept to herself. This wasn't entirely surprising, since those of us who knew her best understood that Cleo wasn't quite gregarious. Still, despite Missy's assurances that it always took some time for dogs to adjust to their new surroundings, I found myself increasingly concerned that maybe we had made the wrong move. Nomi's prison analogy didn't do much to help. Cleo wasn't exactly cut out for the rules of the yard. She'd led a very cushy life, and it didn't take an animal anthropologist to know that she wouldn't take well to being propelled into the jungle of prison life.

Even though I knew we didn't really have any other options, and even as I did my best to relax—going on lengthy trail rides on a rugged mountain bike through the spectacular British Columbian mountains with Krishu strapped into a trailer behind me—I couldn't help but feel an increasing sense of guilt over Cleo. On my third day in Whistler I was feeling real apprehension.

"She's made the turn," Missy happily announced. A new small dog named Billy had arrived that morning and started following Cleo around the play area. Missy said that while at first Cleo seemed irritated by her new sidekick, nipping at Billy and trying to shake him, eventually it seemed to inspire and embolden her. She'd taken to Billy and was now confidently showing him the ropes.

"Really?" I asked her.

"Oh yeah," she insisted. "Trust me, by tomorrow I'm going have a lot more to tell you."

I made the call twenty-four hours later with tremendous anticipation. "So, is Cleo a shot caller as yet?"

"What's a shot caller?" Missy asked, stumped. It was a prison term I had discovered a few years ago while researching online a project that took place, in part, inside a prison. It referred to the leader inside the prison population, the one who often "called the shots" and hence set the culture of the place.

"Forget it," I advised Missy. "How's she doing today?"

"I told you," Missy replied ebulliently. "Billy and Cleo have put together their own little pack. There're a bunch of them, a little pack of small dogs that Cleo is leading around the play area. During some of the structured play we do, they all watch Cleo and try to do the tricks the way she does them."

My heart sank. "Tricks?" This was a dead giveaway. Missy had confused Cleo with another dog. "Cleo?"

"Oh yeah," she answered in her familiar twang. "Your little white mutt is a born leader."

I couldn't help but beam.

"I'm going to have to watch her closely now," Missy confessed. "The larger her group grows, the more the other ones notice. That can cause some friction."

Right, I thought to myself. Prison life. Gangs. Things can easily escalate.

"Don't worry. Cleo doesn't seem the type to cause trouble."

Indeed she didn't. Despite her Napoleon complex, she was unlikely to lead any Bolshevik-like uprising.

I hung up the phone thrilled with what Missy had told me. I tracked Candice down in the spa. "Cleo's got a bitch!" I told her happily, shocking the women giving her a manicure.

. . .

LATER THAT EVENING at dinner, I shared Missy's update with the rest of the family. While during the days we all went our own separate ways, indulging in different activities in and around the resort, even dropping in on Papa's course occasionally, dinner together had emerged as a daily ritual. It was a time to tell stories, let the kids play with one another under the table, and softly wind down the day.

Over the last few months, Cleo had become an increasing topic of conversation. Her antics with Papa, not to mention my quasi insights gleaned from her, gave rise to laughs and rolling eyes, sighs, and smiles. Her latest rise to gangster status back in LA earned her even more accolades. In hindsight, I suppose our Cleo anecdotes had indeed taken an obvious tone. We'd started to talk about Cleo with a fondness that almost felt as if she were no longer with us. Perhaps it was unconscious, a subtle acknowledgment of what we all knew to be true—Cleo was getting old. She had visibly slowed down since passing the decade mark. Candice and I recently both poked around the Internet, uncovering the average life expectancy for mixed breeds like Cleo. All evidence pointed to the fact that she was, like my father liked to say, in the "twilight of her life."

Tara in particular paid close attention whenever Cleo's name came up. Recently she had become aware of the concept of "dog years." That, combined with her increasing focus on arithmetic in school, allowed her to compute that Cleo was well into her seventies by now. Based on the fact that anyone aged more than about eleven was "old" to her, Cleo qualified as ancient. In that context, her reaction when Cleo's name came up that evening was not wholly unexpected. She broke into tears.

Mallika, the ever-attentive mother, took Tara into her arms.

"Is Cleo dying?" Tara cut to the chase.

I interrupted. "No—Cleo's fine. She's totally fine."

She stared at me with tear-filled eyes. "Mamu [the Indian term for uncle], she's getting really old. I can see it. And I think she's going to die soon."

Ever helpless, the adults at the table stared back at Tara in silence.

"Go get your father," my mother instructed me.

I tracked my father down in a conference room, discussing the idea of "peace cells" (the opposite of sleeper cells) with a Swiss couple who worked with the UN. I apologized for interrupting before whispering into my father's ear what was up.

He nodded and rose to his feet. Papa advised the Swiss couple that a family emergency had arisen and he had to tend to it. World peace would have to wait.

"What's wrong?" Papa asked Tara when we returned to the dinner table.

"I don't want Cleo to die," she replied. Just the idea of it unleashed a single tear. "I don't want her to leave us."

Papa didn't miss a beat. "You know, Tara, over the last few weeks I've spent a lot more time with Cleo than I ever had before."

He smiled, thinking through some of their moments over the summer. "And I realized that Cleo has been a real gift for all of us. She really loves us, and she takes all the love we can give her. But like the best gifts, we have to enjoy her while we have her, and not worry about someday in the future when we won't."

Papa brushed the tear away from Tara's cheek. She tried to smile but came up a little short.

"Cleo is a gift from the universe to us. But she's not really ours. We're just here to care for her until someday, hopefully far into the future, the universe will take her back like it does all of us. We just have to be grateful for the time we have together and make sure that we take advantage of every single second because it is the most precious time we have.

"If you can see Cleo in your mind and feel Cleo in your heart, then she'll never really be away from you, right?"

Tara nodded.

"It's better than smelling her or hearing her constantly bark, right?"

This time, Tara burst out laughing. Papa took her into his arms triumphantly.

Tara smiled at her mom, reassuring her that her crisis had been averted, however temporarily. Mallika exhaled with relief, well aware that this was just the start of a great many coming-of-age moments.

It occurred to me, however, that this wasn't just a coming-of-age moment for Tara. It was one for Papa as well. Seeing Tara gaining his affection had of course prompted his other two grandchildren—Leela and Krishu—to seek it as well. Tenuously they now all climbed into his lap and hung on to their grandfather. It was an unlikely portrait, though one the summer had seemed to make familiar. I looked at my mom, curious for her reaction. Now she was the one with watery eyes. Suddenly I suspected that her master summer plan had worked.

For all his many identities—teacher, student, celebrity, doctor, author, Larry King sidekick—family man was a new one for Papa and something he was still getting used to. And yet, he wore it well. It seemed to align with a certain part of him that in moments when he wasn't hustling a best seller, contemplating consciousness, or trying to solve the world's problems, he settled into rather effortlessly.

As Krishu tried to feed Papa a spoonful of banana caramel pie, one of the course attendees passed by our table. He did a double take when he saw Papa sitting there with three little kids climbing all over him.

Papa greeted him and introduced the family. The man was from Colorado, a recent divorcé at the course trying to manage and reconcile the sorrow over his failed marriage.

"It's nice to see you with your family," the man remarked after a few minutes of idle chitchat. "I don't know why that image just never occurred to me."

Papa shrugged and smiled back at him. "Me neither."

AS MUCH AS they say (whoever they are) that parenting is instinctive, it's really not. For me, hunting and gathering never quite felt natural. The notion of protecting and providing, creating a nest egg, drawing up a will, and all of the other behaviors and rituals that went along with fatherhood required learning and getting comfortable with them. Some, to this day, remain far out of my wheelhouse.

And yet there were less actionable feelings linked to parenting that were indeed intuitive to me. Krishu was born three and a half weeks early. As if we weren't prepared for the game changer that parenting entailed, his premature timing ensured that we were absolutely caught with our pants down. For me, this was quite literal,

When Candice nudged me at two a.m. and alerted me that she "thought her water broke," I nudged her back and said that she probably "thought wrong." (In my defense, I was still half-asleep.) Of course she was right, and it soon dawned on me that we were at the point of no return. In a panicked frenzy, I leaped from the bed and spurred into action, rounding up whatever I could think of to throw into a bag and get us to the hospital. It was only once we were in car that Candice remarked that I seemed to have forgotten something.

"I put Cleo's food out," I replied confidently. My parenting chops were already kicking in, as if not allowing the dog to starve to death was a great achievement.

"Nope." She pointed downward. I followed her finger and noticed that I was only wearing boxers.

Thirty minutes later, Candice and I (wearing a nice pair of Polo sweats) found ourselves in the maternity ward of Santa Monica–UCLA Medical Center, trying to make small talk while struggling to drown out the sounds of a wailing woman down the hall—"Get this thing the @#$% out of me!!!!"

"Don't worry," I assured Candice like a complete male imbecile with no idea what I was talking about. "I'm sure your delivery will be quick and painless."

Yeah, right.

Twenty-two and a half hours later, our baby son was born. Having witnessed firsthand what Candice endured to deliver him, it remains a wonder to me every single day that she loves the two of us.

It's only been a couple of years, but I like to think that Candice and I have done a pretty bang-up job. Still, it's hard—no, impossible—to tell a two-year-old to value anything in his life. But I regularly do so anyway with my son. Even if he doesn't know so now, he'll one day realize that Cleo has been an important influence in his life. Not just because of the way she loves and licks him, but because by her very unbounded being she demonstrates some of the most important qualities that he'll ever learn.

More than what she's taught me or Papa, the lessons Cleo is imparting to Krishu—at an age when every day the universe is rapidly imprinting itself onto his consciousness—are among the most precious he will ever take away. I say this with all the perspective of being a "son of" when I know in my heart that one day I will be even more proud to say I am the "father of."

SOMEWHERE IN THE midst of the fourth or fifth day of Papa's courses, the attendees really hit their stride. This was the portion of the course that was most valuable for the majority of people, where they could examine both their own personal dilemmas as well as larger planetary ones with a sobriety that was at the same time rooted in a much greater perspective of the connectivity of all things. By that stage, that connectivity was experiential, not simply conceptual. That collective experience of peeling back layers of one's self in the open and trusted atmosphere of the course created a uniquely nurturing and inspiring energy. Even I, the cynic in the family, recognized that.

This was the same phase of the course where Papa also hit his groove. That same inspiring energy fueled him. His lectures took on an added edge. His insights pushed new bounds. Not much—the news of failing health care, a tumbling economy, fiery rhetoric between imperialists and terrorists that plagued the outside world—could really stall him. He was *go go go* whether it was dealing with how to help individuals tap their own consciousness and heal themselves or take on those larger global crises and with the help of others think up creative solutions.

Perhaps the only thing that could slow him down—both literally and figuratively—was a stalled gondola, which is exactly what happened as he, Krishu, and I rode up a steep mountain peak.

"Now what do we do?" Papa asked as we hung about two hundred feet over a dried ski slope, our gondola gently rocking back and forth.

"There's not much we really can do unless you are MacGyver," I replied.

"Who's MacGyver?" He looked at me, confused.

I shook my head. "I guess we just have to wait."

Krishu, meanwhile, seemed unperturbed by our predicament. Moving or not, the gondola itself was a singular adventure to him.

"Look." He pointed out the window of the enclosed compartment. Awe washed over his expression in the form of a smile that could power all New York City.

Papa and I followed his little finger to see what he was pointing at. I could make out nothing in particular. The mountain we were climbing dipped into a valley where our resort and a few other posh properties sat. After a few miles of settled land, the mountains picked up again and climbed steeply toward snowcapped peaks that scraped the sky. The sun had set behind those peaks, but shards of light still shot upward, creating an orange and purple haze.

"What, Krishu? What do you see?"

"That!" Krishu gestured with his finger again more forcefully. I followed it again, staring out at the vast expanse of sky.

Papa was doing the same thing now. We both squinted, trying to figure the mystery out. "What's he pointing at?"

Suddenly it occurred to me. I sat back on the padded bench laughing.

"Nothing. He's pointing at nothing."

"What do you mean?" Papa shook his head, still not getting it.

"Or everything." I shrugged my shoulders. "I guess it depends on your perspective."

Papa looked again out the window. He took in the mountain dipping into the valley, the expanse of land, the mountains opposite us that climbed steeply toward snowy peaks, the sunset behind them, and the shard of light that formed the orange and purple haze. The vast magic of planet Earth, the mythical domain where those snowy peaks scraped the sky, *that's* what Krishu was pointing at.

At last he got it. "Fantastic." Papa nodded.

Papa took Krishu into his lap. "You're a genius." He tickled him affectionately. He turned to me. "He's a real *rishi*, a seer."

Krishu took the compliment with his trademark humility. He had already moved on from his last revelation and was pointing down below. Papa and I once again followed his finger, this time determined to spot his insight and not have to get too existential about it.

This time, however, we didn't need guru glasses to see what Krishu had spotted. A midsize black bear clumsily picked through a pile of sticks and leaves on the ground. Krishu became more animated as it dawned on him that this was a real, live bear.

"Dada, bear!" he exclaimed.

"Wow!" Papa replied excitedly, now well trained in the grandfather arts.

His glee confirmed, Krishu just stared at the bear wide-eyed with wonder.

Papa too remained silent. A similar sort of wide-eyed awe fixed on his expression. But he wasn't watching the bear. He was watching Krishu.

"You know," Papa addressed me, not taking his eyes off Krishu, "this will be your challenge as a father.

"How do you preserve and protect this sense of innocence and unboundedness as Krishu grows up and confronts a world that demands the opposite from him? Conformity nags at us all."

He turned in his seat and looked at me. "It's not easy."

Was he talking about me? I wondered. Or himself?

Krishu remained mesmerized by the bear below. But like he often did when he noticed that others around him were talking to anyone but him, he tried to redirect his grandfather's attention back to himself.

"Look, Dada." He pointed once more down below.

"The bear is eating." Papa nodded, impressed. "I see it."

"Yeah," Krishu concurred. "I see rhino and tiger." His eyes went wide with added excitement.

"Wow." Papa played along.

"And elephant and penguin," Krishu continued. If you followed his eyes, you could see that for Krishu, the rhino, tiger, elephant, and penguin were just as real as the bear. Like Cleo, unboundedness for him was not a spiritual quality, not some ideal that he had to reach for or integrate into his life. It was a state of being. How long would it last? The world and I would work together to make it linger as long as possible. That's the best that I could do.

The gondola lurched as the whir of the cable sounded and pulled us forward. We were back up and running. Krishu started waving good-bye to his friends below and searching for new ones as the mountainside got steeper.

"Did Mom tell you what I'm doing?" Papa changed the topic.

I shook my head, unsure what he was referring to.

"I'm becoming vegetarian and I am going to Thailand to spend a month being a monk."

I stared at him blankly. The vegetarian part I had heard before. Many times. The monk part? That was a new addition.

"One month at a monastery. Just meditation and a begging bowl, living off the charity of others."

Wow. I didn't really know what else to say.

Papa, of course, didn't need me nor anyone else to keep the conversation going. "I need time to think about what I really want to be remembered for."

I nodded.

He smiled as if he'd just listened to what he said. "And I need time to think why I really care to be remembered at all."

THE FOLLOWING MORNING before breakfast I sat in my room and made my phone calls. I called the doggy day care in LA and Nomi actually picked up the phone.

"Hey bro," he greeted me. "I told you, your dog is like an OG. You know what that means, right?"

I was hip enough to know that it meant "original gangster." It was a term back from the day when rap music first made its hard impression, and it denoted a certain urban respect, a fusion of godfather-like status with ghetto Zen.

"Nah bro." Nomi laughed. "Not when it comes to Cleo *Chopra*. She ain't no gangster. She's an original guru, man."

This time I was the one laughing.

"She's got quite the crew," Nomi advised me. Cleo's posse of small dogs had swelled in size.

"Tell your dad he'd better watch his back."

I thanked Nomi and told him I'd call the following day to check in again.

"Whatever, bro. Cleo's leading us on a pilgrimage to Joshua Tree. Original guru is ultimate guru."

I smiled to myself as I made my way to the small business lounge that sat just beside my parents' hotel room. They were on a special VIP floor where perks such as free breakfast came with the room. Unfortunately for them, they had not counted on our commandeering the premises with our extended clan. After some initial resistance, they'd relented and we'd essentially turned the place into our own private dining room.

This morning, Mallika had requested we all arrive promptly at eight a.m. because Tara had an announcement she wanted to make. I knew not to cross my sister and arrived with seconds to spare. Everyone else—including both my parents—sat attentively awaiting Tara's news. Mallika handed her the floor.

"I'm, um," Tara started nervously.

"Just say it!" Leela egged her on.

"Say it," Krishu echoed Leela in his chirpy little voice.

"Okayyyy." Tara eyed Tweedledee and Tweedledum. "I'm getting a puppy!" she blurted. Her eyes sparkled with excitement.

"Tell them the deal we cut," Mallika prompted her.

Tara nodded. "Leela and I promised my mom to clean our rooms every week, not fight, do our homework every night, and watch less TV."

Mallika nodded at me and winked.

Tara's excitement knew no bounds. She had been nagging her parents for a puppy since as far back as any of us could remember. Her war of attrition had finally paid off.

For the rest of the day, we bandied about potential names. Favorites included Delhi (Sumant's), Chutney (my mom's), Moksha (Papa's), Jedi (Candice's), Rumi (Mallika's), Fuzz Ball (Leela's), and Tom Brady (mine). Krishu meanwhile was conflicted. Naturally he assumed that any new dog coming into the family would follow Cleo's footsteps—literally. Hence "Cleo 2" was his presumptive selection.

Gradually we did manage to convince him that the new dog,

while being a sibling of Cleo's the same way he was of Tara and Leela, should have its own name and identity.

That's when his new favorite inexplicably emerged: "Trash Can."

Over the course of the next few days, as our glorious vacation—and summer—drew to a close, we all got more and more excited about the new imminent member of the family. Mallika became increasingly determined that she would follow a strict and rigid regimen to ensure the new puppy was trained from the start and avoided all the many bad habits that another family favorite had taken on. Candice and I played along, supporting her false hopes and smirking at each other knowingly behind her back.

Curiously it was Tara—initially the instigator of the whole effort—who seemed to be headed in the other direction. Always the contemplative one, she grew more quiet as the days passed and the time got closer to actually getting the puppy when we all got back to LA.

"Gotham Mamu." She approached me at the airport as we waited to board our flight home.

There was a conflict in her voice. I could tell that she was in deep thought on something. Papa too, sitting beside me reading a magazine, could hear it. He turned to her, instantly concerned.

"What's the matter?"

"Well, I just . . ." Tears formed in her eyes. "I just want Cleo to know that no matter what, even when we have a new puppy, I'll never forget that she was my first dog. And I'll always love her in a special way."

Relieved, Papa and I smiled simultaneously.

"You know, Tara"—I took her into my arms—"there's no rule that says you can't love two dogs as much as possible at the same time."

This time the relief was apparent with her. "I was thinking," she said with an expression that suggested she actually had and quite considerably, "that since Cleo will be the new puppy's big sister, she could teach him, you know, *everything.*"

I nodded slowly. My sister was going to kill me.

"I think that's a great idea," Papa interrupted. "Cleo certainly has a lot to teach us all."